THE SACRED NUMBERS
OF INITIATION

The Sacred Numbers of Initiation
Lars Muhl

First published in the UK in 2023 by Watkins,
an imprint of Watkins Media Limited
Unit 11, Shepperton House,
83–93 Shepperton Road
London N1 3DF

enquiries@watkinspublishing.com

1 2 3 4 5 6 7 8 9 10

Special thanks to Naleea Landmann for editing

Printed in the United Kingdom by TJ Books Ltd

A CIP record for this book is available from the British Library

ISBN: 978-1-78678-801-6 (Hardback)
ISBN: 978-1-7867-880-3 (eBook)

www.watkinspublishing.com

LARS MUHL

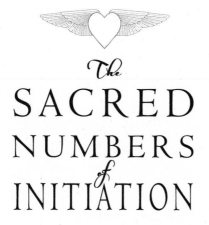

SACRED NUMBERS of INITIATION

An Ancient
Essene Numerology System

WATKINS
Sharing Wisdom
Since 1893

Heavenly Source,
You who are everywhere.
Blessed be Your sacred Vibration.
Kindle in us the fire of Your Love,
here and now and forevermore.
Open our hearts to the Power of Compassion
and free us from the fetters
with which we bind ourselves and each other.
Lead us out of the darkness,
let us rest in our Higher Self
so that we can be close to You.
Forgive us and let us forgive
until our actions are at one
with Your Holy Instant.
Amen.

CONTENTS

OPEN HEART

REVEALING THE CONCEALED

The numerology system I first presented in my book *The Wisdom of a Broken Heart* was never brought to its final conclusion. I was shown this supposedly ancient Sanskrit numerology system by Mar Van der Velde, who owned Les Contes in the Pyrenees, where I used to camp when I was working on my own or with groups in the area around Montségur back in 2006. Mar and his lovely wife Leni were like parents to me, always there to support me and lead me in the right direction. I don't know where exactly Mar learned to do the numerology system; I only know that it was incredibly accurate whenever he "read" somebody using the system. Since then, I have worked with it on and off until I had to follow the call to investigate it more. And when I did this, nothing seemed more natural than to apply my knowledge of the Essenes and their insights of their Aramaic and Hebrew alphabet to the system, and, in that way, develop a whole new approach to it.

With *The Sacred Numbers of Initiation*, I therefore offer a new updated version of that old system. The "Broken Heart" still refers to the process of spiritual awakening and the opening of the Heart, revealing the concealed Kingdom of Heaven within – through any experience that takes one out of the perceived comfort zone of the personality, may it be in regards to a relationship with a loved one, an illness, a spiritual suffering about the state of the world or any other kind of pain that works as a fuel for awakening.

WALK THE TALK

The aim of *The Sacred Numbers of Initiation* is to inspire you and give you an idea of the spiritual qualities and potentials you carry within you in this incarnation – which can develop and manifest when you become aware of their existence. It is crucial to acknowledge that you *are* already Enlightened and that this incarnation is all about being aware of it, taking responsibility for it and unfolding it in your everyday life. Simply put, the words attached to the numbers want to inspire you to "walk the talk".

THE MELCHIZEDEK LINEAGE

The text for the 22 "Seed", or incarnation, numbers and the Bible verses and other quotations that follow in this book reflect the gematria and philosophy of the Essenes, with their roots reaching toward their true founder and first Teacher of Righteousness, Melchizedek (King of Righteousness), the first Priest-King of Salem (Jerusalem). This mystery tradition was later refined through the prophet Samuel and the prophets Elias and Elisha in the School of Prophets on Mount Carmel. Five hundred years later it was practiced by the Essene Brother and Sisterhood at Qumran by the Dead Sea, in Israel; at their temple in Heliopolis and at their school of Therapeutae, at Lake Mareotis, in Egypt; and last, but not least, in their desert-settlements west of Damascus, in Syria.

THE HOLY MOUNTAIN

Mount Carmel is a twenty-four-mile-long mountain range in Galilee, northern Israel, which overlooks the Mediterranean Sea. As far back as 1400 BC, Egyptian Pharaoh Thutmose III considered the mount to be a holy site. Pythagoras visited the mountain and regarded it as one of the most holy. According to Roman historian Tacitus, an oracle resided on Mount Carmel that Emperor Vespian consulted during his reign. Tacitus also mentions that there was an altar there – an altar without any images and without a temple building around it.

THE NAME OF THE ESSENES

The Essenes didn't refer to themselves as "Essenes", but were named such by later sources. They called themselves *"Osei ha-Torah"* or *"Osseenes"*, meaning "Keepers of the Covenant", "Those who manifest the Law" or "Those of the Way of the Covenant". In our time, they would be recognized as "Those who walk the talk".

In the Melchizedek/Essene tradition, the Heavenly Source of All Being created everything through the 22 letters of the Aramaic and Hebrew alphabet, which, with their different images, sounds and qualities, represent the etheric archetypes. These archetypes must be acknowledged, understood and established within, before the actual manifestation of their qualities can take place in the physical world. Insights from this tradition are embedded in the cryptic words of *The Gospel of Phillip* and *The Gospel of Thomas,* which were found in Nag Hammadi in Egypt in 1945, together with a whole library of so-called gnostic gospels. Although written in Coptic, these gospels are believed to have originally come from Syria and been written in Syrian Aramaic. The gnostic movement was an extension of the Essene and Therapeutae mystery traditions, and the scribes of the Dead Sea Scrolls were also the scribes behind many of the gospels, acts and treatises being circulated after Yeshua's ascension. Some of these were among the Nag Hammadi findings, while *The Gospel of John* and other parts of their writings ended up in the New Testament. Be aware that Yeshua was the long-awaited new incarnation of the Essenes' beloved Teacher of

Righteousness. After the destruction of the Temple in Jerusalem and the University at Qumran by the Romans in 90 AD, the Essenes went underground and continued to pass on their knowledge and insights to a select few. In that way, the tradition survived through the ages within some of the gnostic groups that dedicated themselves to the sharing of knowledge and wisdom, culminating in 1200 AD with the Cathar movement in France, and different Sufi and Kabbalist movements in Spain, Syria and Israel.

"Truth did not come into the world naked; rather, it came in prototypes and images: the world will not accept it in any other way. Rebirth exists along with an image of rebirth: by means of this image one must be truly reborn. Which image? Resurrection! And image must arise by means of image. By means of this image, the Bridal Chamber and its image must embark upon the realm of Truth, that is, embark upon the return. Not only must those who produce the names of the Father, Son and Holy Spirit do so, but also those who have acquired these. If someone does not acquire them, the name too will be taken from that person."

(*Gospel of Phillip 59:9-21*)

You can find the images of Truth (22), Resurrection (20), Bridal Chamber (6) and Holy Spirit (21) mentioned in the quote just given, together with the rest of the 22 archetypes in *The Sacred Numbers of Initiation*. In the *Gospel of Thomas*, we can read about how Yeshua viewed images:

> "Yeshua said: 'The images are manifest to man, but the Light in them remains concealed in the image of the Light of the Father. He will become manifest, but His image will be concealed by His Light.'"

> "Yeshua said: 'When you see your likeness, you rejoice. But when you see your true image, which came into being before you, and which neither die nor become manifest, how much you will have to bear!'"

> (*Gospel of Thomas*, logion 83 & 84)

Here, Yeshua is talking about the image of the Heavenly Source of All Being in which we were all created, and of which we all carry a small portion within. When we are not allowing this Light to shine freely, but are hiding it in the darkness of our ignorance, our true image will not manifest. The responsibility that comes with manifesting our true image is what holds most people back from realizing it and taking it upon themselves. This is the only real secret of life and the hereafter, which must be understood in all its fullness. To the Essenes and the Therapeutae, the Aramaic alphabet, with its numbers and images, was part of a highly revered science, which it is almost impossible for outsiders to grasp the extent of without having access to the metaphorical meanings and wisdom of the archetypes contained therein. Hopefully the release of this little book will help to change that.

"You are the Light of the world! A city built upon a hill cannot be concealed. And they do not light a lamp and place it under a bushel; but upon a light-stand and it gives light to all that are in the house. Let your Light shine before men, that they may see and glorify the works of the Heavenly Source of All Being."

(*Gospel of Matthew 5:14-16*)

THE ANCIENT ORACLES

The Oracle of Delphi was served by twelve Moon Priestesses. Each Priestess represented a specific month of the year. Anyone who visited the oracle in search for an answer had to enter through a portal, above which were engraved the words "Know Thyself". By following a path that went underground into a maze of narrow corridors, the inquirer was taken to an opening carved into the stone wall known as the "Mouth of the Oracle". The inquirer had to stand in front of the opening and voice his or her question, which, through a sophisticated system of channels, was transported to the Priestess waiting at the other end. After a period of contemplation, whether short or long, the Priestess would deliver her answer, which would always be of a cryptic nature. Why? Because the true purpose of the oracle was to awaken the inquirer's own intuition.

The answer was meant to be like a feather of possibility and promise floating in the air, pointing toward the inquirer's own inner guidance, which would be explored and contemplated by the inquirer as he or she was finding their way back through the maze, up into the reality of everyday life.

Such are the workings of any genuine oracle, to open up hearts, to awaken and to guide, but always without spelling it out.

The question that all searchers for answers should ask themselves is: "What do I want to achieve with this question?", "Why am I asking it?" or, said in another way: "Why ask a question if you already know the answer?" The inquirer must always be prepared before approaching an oracle.

FROM THE WORLD
OF QUESTIONS

We live in a society in which the developed intellect is revered as the highest level of consciousness that humans can reach. And the intellect is certainly an indispensable tool when it comes to reflecting, processing and controlling data. Yet natural science is not able to explain human consciousness, let alone the multidimensional consciousness of the Heavenly Source of All Being.

While natural scientists are conducting tests in their labs, collecting data from the physical world, and weighing and measuring this, spiritual scientists are gathering their results through personal experiences from the world within themselves by means of spiritual practices.

One of the reasons for many of the problems we face in the world today lies in humankind's often one-dimensional attitude toward life and what constitutes a human being. When we don't take our spiritual potential into consideration, but revere only natural science, with all its limitations, as the answer to any question, we end up in a reality where technology rules and the next big thing will be some kind of artificial intelligence.

When we search for answers only via the world of intellectual questions, we will find only limited solutions to our problems. In order to find genuine wisdom and long-lasting solutions, we must leave the intellect, with all its limitations, in order to approach the world of spiritual answers. This bypassing of the intellect is achieved by doing spiritual work, prayer and meditation that frees us from all personal and existential noise. Only in this way is it possible for a drop of water to expand its awareness and consciousness of the ocean.

SYMBOL & PROPHECY

THE ORACLE OF LETTERS AND NUMBERS

The Heavenly Source of All Being (God) is pure consciousness and creational love. The language of the universe is energy. The language of the angels is empathy and prophecy. The language of humankind is signs and symbols. The significance of signs and symbols depends on our ability to manifest love, empathy and prophecy in the world. If humankind fails to manifest this love, compassion and prophetic sense, the language of the angels and the universe remains hidden, and this is the cause of what we call evil in the world.

The language the Essenes used most frequently in their work was Aramaic, and there was a good reason for this. The Aramaic language expresses transpersonal psychology so completely that the word order alone can simultaneously describe the interaction between mindset, acknowledgement, sensory perception, common sense, judgment, ability to understand, and our attitudes and behavior. It neither differentiates between the mental, physical, emotional and spiritual, nor between cause and effect. The root of every word and concept is neutral, but is activated and given meaning by adding the suffixes "-ta" or "-oota". These express an energy that activates the ether. In Aramaic, a word or concept can have many meanings that don't always seem to be in agreement with each other. But, unlike other languages where a word with two meanings demands that one of them be excluded, all the meanings in Aramaic are active simultaneously. The language, therefore, has an openness that embraces existence in a life-affirming way and encourages interpretation and narration. Not only the meaning of a word but also its sound is an important factor in understanding why Aramaic was an important instrument in the Essenes' work. Particular words, as well as each of their letters, possess healing powers. And each letter represents a number, which again constitutes frequencies with different spiritual qualities and healing properties.

The Essenes were educated in the science of Aramaic and Hebrew symbols, graphic characters, sounds and numbers. The psychology behind the Aramaic language forms the foundation for the way of thinking in this book, and also for the translations and interpretations of the quotations from the Gospels. The origin of the Aramaic language cannot be traced; we only know that it is related to Sanskrit and that it has formed the basis for the Arabic and Hebrew languages. There is a legend that says it was the angels, at the dawn of time, that brought the Aramaic language to Earth so that humans would be able to understand the voice and sound of the Heavenly Source of All Being through it.

Numbers reveal everything. Through them, we can attain insight into hidden mysteries. The mystery schools of the Essenes and Therapeutae practiced numerology, and the chart overleaf gives an example of a gematria numerology system that goes back to ancient times and through which one can read in the *Book of Life*. Needless to say that the system should be taken with a pinch of salt. Use it to get a general understanding of the reasons for and meaning of the incarnation of the Soul. It is best to regard the numbers, and what they wish to portray, in an archetypical light. Don't take the interpretations literally, but rather let yourself be inspired by them and let them awaken and communicate with your subconscious.

HOW TO MAKE A CHART

Example 1:

The date of birth – in this case 11th July, 1968 – is entered into the "Birth" line of the system, as shown opposite. After this, numbers are entered vertically, with the individual digits of each number in the horizontal line added together to get the number for the line below, other than for the master numbers 11, 22 and 33, the digits of which cannot be added together. For the line representing the period from "15–30" years, 11 and 7 therefore remain as 11 and 7, while 19 becomes 10, and 68 becomes 14. For the next line, representing "30–45", 11 and 7 are entered again, while 10 becomes 1, and 14 becomes 5. For the line representing "45–60", 11 and 7 become 18, and 1 and 5 become 6. In the "Beyond" sphere, representing age 60 until the end of the incarnation, 18 and 6 are added together to give 24. And the digits of 24 are then added together to give the "Seed" of this person's Soul: $2+4 = 6$.

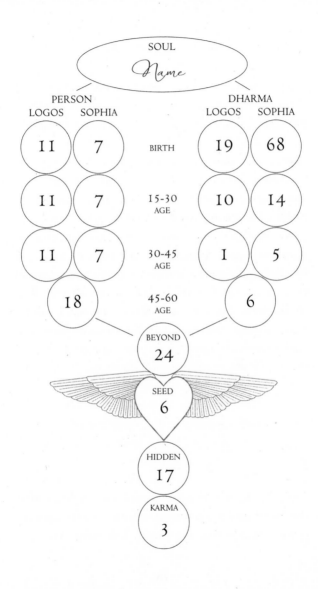

The "Karma" number emerges by going back through the whole chart to see which numbers between 1 and 9 are not present. The presence of a 14, for example, means that both 1 and 4 are present already and therefore aren't "Karma" numbers. In this chart, only the number 3 is missing. But when more than one number is missing, they should each be listed and considered individually (see p.30).

If all numbers are present, the person in question is not characterized by karmic challenges in their present incarnation. This doesn't mean that he or she is not challenged in any way. The challenges are just not of a karmic nature, meaning that they are not rooted in past experiences. The challenges that need to be met are to be found in the "Dharma" section of the chart.

THE SEED

The "Seed" number represents the qualities that the Soul has brought with it into this incarnation — the essence that the entity will have access to throughout its entire life if it recognizes it and takes care of it. The "Karma" stands for the themes with which the Soul will be confronted, and which it will have to work with in one or more ways.

PERSON & DHARMA – LOGOS & SOPHIA

At the top left of the chart, under "Person", are two vertical columns labelled "Logos" (representing thought and masculinity) and "Sophia" (representing feelings and femininity). These show the qualities and potentialities of the personality. At the top right, under "Dharma", are two columns that show the duties and challenges that the Soul will have to work on at different times during the incarnation.

From the 15th to 30th year of life, the personality of the Soul in question is under the influence of the numbers 11 and 7, while its dharma aspect is concerned with the numbers 10 and 14.

As time goes by and the Soul's personality matures, synthesis is eventually created between "Logos" and "Sophia", starting at the age of 45. Here, the personal qualities in "Logos" and "Sophia" merge in 18, while issues still requiring work, both with regard to thoughts ("Logos") and feelings ("Sophia"), are transformed into 6.

From age 60 and beyond – represented by the "Beyond" line – qualities and work-related matters merge together and become 24. This is beautiful proof of how, despite all our opposites, we do in the end mature and become One with our tasks and challenges.

READING THE CHART

The first number of interest is the "Seed". It represents the very essence and skills of your Soul in its present incarnation – the very essence of you.

The next is your "Karma". It almost has the same role as the ascending sign in astrology. It represents what you are trying to achieve and what you want to present to the world, or something that you have to face in this incarnation (often through a partner or a friend).

Next, pay attention to the four numbers of your birth date. As you can see in the chart, there is a "Person" section and a "Dharma" section, each of which is separated into "Logos" (representing thoughts and masculinity) and "Sophia" (representing feelings and femininity).

The "Person" section represents your qualities and potentials at different stages of life, while the "Dharma" section represents the duties and issues that you should work on at different stages.

The "Logos" in the "Person" section is essential to you on a personal level, while the "Sophia" in this section is pointing to a more collective frequency.

In the "Dharma" section, this is opposite, as the "Logos" is representing the collective frequency, while the "Sophia" is representing the personal.

Please read the explanations for all four numbers in the pages that follow in order to get a feeling of the exact qualities and spiritual frequencies available at your time of birth. The most *personally* interesting numbers, however, are "Person" / "Logos" and "Dharma" / "Sophia".

ON PAGES 174—175
YOU WILL FIND
TWO BLANK CHARTS
TO COPY AND PRINT

Example 2:

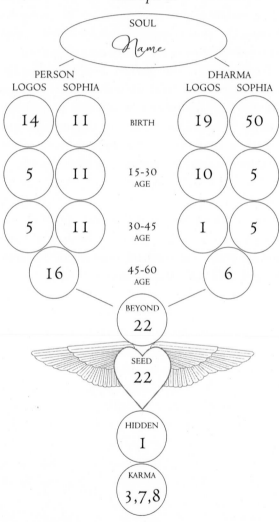

Next, focus on the numbers attached to your age right now. How are your qualities in "Person" matching the challenges in "Dharma"? Read every number and start contemplating the texts.

ATTENTION: When reading the texts, be sure to contemplate the quotations – both biblical and other – that come with each number from 1 to 22, and 33. They are essential on a deep level, connecting you to the eternal path of the Melchizedek Order.

THE HIDDEN NUMBER

When the Dead Sea Scrolls were found in the caves around the ruins of the Essenes' old university at Qumran in 1947, the work of collecting all the pieces in the gigantic puzzle of the many fragmented scrolls began under the leadership of the Catholic priests Father de Vaux and Father Milik. Other scholars included John Strugnell, Frank Cross and John Allegro. But it was the Jewish historian and scholar Hugh Schonfield who discovered the Atbash cipher used by the Essenes in one of their works known as *The Assumption of Moses*. In this text, he found a peculiar name, TAXO, that didn't make any sense until he applied the aforementioned Atbash cipher and the name ASAPH appeared. Asaph was a psalmist, singer, stargazer, healer and seer at King Solomon's court, and Schonfield connected him to the Essenes as an incarnation of their Messiah, their Teacher of Righteousness.

If you apply the Atbash cipher to the "Seed" you will find the mirror number in your chart, also called the "Hidden" number. This contains an unknown message from your subconscious that will add more depth to the understanding of your path.

If your incarnation, or "Seed", number is 1, your mirror, or "Hidden", number will be 22; if the former is 2, the latter will be 21, and so on – see below. The "Hidden" number is given in grey under each "Seed" number later in the book.

1 = 22	12 = 11
2 = 21	13 = 10
3 = 20	14 = 9
4 = 19	15 = 8
5 = 18	16 = 7
6 = 17	17 = 6
7 = 16	18 = 5
8 = 15	19 = 4
9 = 14	20 = 3
10 = 13	21 = 2
11 = 12	22 = 1

The numbers 11, 22 and 33 are known as "master numbers". They have been so named because they have greater but also more challenging potential than other numbers. They have a high vibration frequency, are difficult to deal with, and require time, maturity and great effort when trying to integrate them into the personality.

11 represents vision, 22 combines vision and action, while 33 offers guidance to the world.

If one carries a master number, one has to be prepared for many tests. The murder of the US president John F. Kennedy happened on 22nd November, 1963. Many other disasters have occurred on dates that contain an 11, a 22 or both.

The bearer of a master number has much potential, but also carries a great responsibility. And many 11s, 22s and 33s pull back from accepting that responsibility. An 11 who is not ready to face his/her responsibility, or runs away from it, will struggle as a 2, just as a 22 who doesn't face his or her responsibility will have a hard time as a 4, and a 33 will be reduced to a 6.

THE GEMATRIA OF YOUR NAME

Take the first letter of your first name and find its number on the opposite page. If your name is Maria, the first letter is Mem, which is number 13. Then do the same with your surname.

The energy, vibration and frequency of the letters in your name (especially your first name) is very powerful. Compare the information given through it with the information given through your "Seed" number and you will get a pretty clear picture of your potentials and purpose in this life on a higher plane.

TAROT AND NUMBERS

As a last treat you should find all the main numbers of your numerology chart and match them with the identical cards of the Great Arcana of a Tarot deck. Line the cards up on a table in front of you and contemplate the images on the cards.

I can personally recommend the 6th edition of *The Alchemical Tarot – Renewed* by Robert M. Place. This is the only deck that I know of where the Fool is the 0 that travels through the

LETTER	NAME		LETTER	NAME	
1 א	Aleph	A, E, O, U	12 ל	Lamed	L
2 ב	Beit	B	13 מ	Mem	M
3 ג	Gimel	G	14 נ	Nun	N
4 ד	Daleth	D	15 ס	Samech	S
5 ה	Heh	H	16 ע	Ayin	
6 ו	Vav	V, W	17 פ	Peh	P, F
7 ז	Zayin	Z	18 צ	Tzadik	TZ, TS
8 ח	Chet		19 ק	Qoph	Q
9 ט	Teth	T	20 ר	Resh	R
10 י	Yod	Y, I, J	21 ש	Shin	SH
11 כ	Kaph	K, C	22 ת	Tav	TH

22 archetypical forces in the Major Arcana – something that I always felt was how it ought to be.

The deck's general focus is the merging of the Sacred Feminine and the Sacred Masculine, which is also the main focus of this book, *The Sacred Numbers of Initiation*.

TO BE READ BEFORE
YOU READ YOUR NUMBERS

As said before: Your numbers are not telling the truth of who you are. Instead they are telling you what you *could* be, what you can aspire to, the potentials that await you, and what can be achieved if you are willing to make an effort. Remember, you are already Enlightened, but you need to take responsibility for it, realize it and manifest this Light/Consciousness in everyday life. You need to "walk the talk"!

Many modern oracles are offering lofty promises. These can be the sweet music we long to hear, but way too often this keeps us locked up in fancy illusions, hindering us from taking the next step toward our true calling in this incarnation. Always remember that two people could share the same number, with the same form and sound, but with totally different melodies. Each letter and number has more than one frequency. It all depends on where you came from when you entered the present incarnation, and the choices you make along the way. All oracles, be it *The I Ching*, *The Tarot* or *The Sacred Numbers of Initiation*, are only guidelines, pointing you in a certain direction. In the end, it's your choices and your perception of the messages given to you through the oracles that determine where you end up. The more present and balanced you are in the moment of consulting your oracle, the more certain you can be that you will be directed toward the World of Answers. There, you will find your own Inner Guide mirrored and explained. You are carrying the Sacred Seed of Truth, Love and Compassion within. *The Sacred Numbers of Initiation* will simply help you to walk in the direction of this sacred trinity.

THE ETERNAL LANGUAGE

Symbols, metaphors and archetypical images are the languages needed in order to understand the earthly incarnation. A time will come when the incarnated Soul realizes that this symbolic language is the only way humanity can experience and express ways of breaking through its physical limitations and take the next step forward toward the inner, holographic and multidimensional levels. The Soul already contains this universal language within itself – it just needs to be activated.

The "Seed" texts in the pages that follow are inspirational words from the lineage of the Melchizedek/Essene Brother and Sisterhood, received when meditating on each letter and number of the Aramaic alphabet.

"You yourself are the abyss opening below you as well as the bridge you must cross. You are the path you must follow and the mountain you have to climb. You are the cave you must find and enter. And when you rest there, you'll realize that you are the cloud above you in the sky, that you are the rain falling and evaporating again; you are the drop of water that will soon become the ocean. That is when you will know the Heavenly Source of All Being."

(The ⊙ Manuscript)

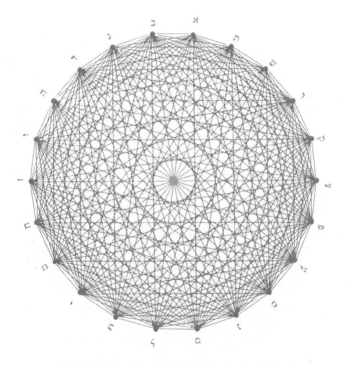

The Essenes believed that the Heavenly Source of All Being created everything through the 22 letters of the Aramaic/Hebrew alphabet. Interconnecting the letters with each other, the Etheric net of Light/Consciousness was created, constituting the matrix on which the physical reality was manifested.

THE SACRED NUMBERS
OF INITIATION

The text that follows gives suggestions as to the interpretation of the "Seed" numbers 1 to 22, as well as the master number 33. These are followed by short explanatory statements of the numbers from 23 to 100, as well as 200, 300, 345, 365 and 400. When you are working with a number consisting of two digits, you have to see what each digit stands for as well as the sum of them.

Just as it is not the individual note in a piece of music that constitutes the whole, it is not the individual number in itself, according to the ancient numerology system, that makes up the whole. A number's origin as well as its subsequent destination adds context to its uniqueness.

6 has just left 5 and is now on its way toward 7. So many possibilities for interpretation lie in this

understanding as our attention is drawn again and
again to seek cohesion.

A note to the prayers attached to each letter:

Thanks to Naleea Landmann, the prayers of Psalm 119
have been paraphrased, using the old Midrash tradition.
Each verse has been opened toward awareness of, and
access to, the living vibration of the Heavenly Source
of All Being, replacing the concept of a judgmental and
punishing father figure and transforming all corresponding
conditional appeals and polarized deals. When you read
and contemplate the prayers, it is important to take into
consideration that the Essenes were masters of metaphors.

Terms like "the arrogant" and "those who forgot/deny"
are not only referring to seemingly outer opponents, but
just as much to the arrogance, forgetfulness and denial
within the praying brother or sister themselves, leaving the
question: What good is an armor of the Heart, protecting
you against exterior enemies, when the most dangerous
attackers, the shadows of your ego, strike from within?

---

0 - THE VOID

The not-yet-created, endless potential. That which
embraces everything, but is, in itself, nothing. The
great, contemplative force, which awaits the point
of creation and is the force of activation when
joined to the number 1. All created things originate
from 0 and return to it once more. Tarot: *The Fool*.

I

ALEPH

UNITY AND MASTERY
The Messiah

(A, E, O, U) Fire. The Sun. The Archangel *Metatron*, "The Angel of the Covenant". Unity. The Monad. The Infinite Point. Teacher of Righteousness. The Instrument of Truth. Seed. Semen. Essence. Matrix.

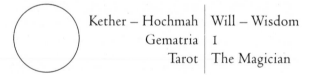

	Kether – Hochmah	Will – Wisdom
	Gematria	1
	Tarot	The Magician

Beginning. The Original. The Creative Force. Power through self-control. The Messenger. Desire into Manifestation. Creativity. Protection and Goodness. Primordial Force. The Masculine Principle. Individualist. Leader. A fire that burns but does not destroy.

With a strong sense of self-worth and self-confidence, a number 1 finds it difficult to accept criticism as he/she considers him/herself perfect. A 1 will usually expect, and earn, the respect of others, and has a tendency to control and organize everything around them. They thrive when at the center of events, accept nothing but the best and tend to be stubborn and, at times, arrogant.

1's intense energy is best used on giving and creativity. These things make them feel alive and vigorous. When 1 is drawn toward selfishness, the result is pain and imbalance, and they will experience resistance and setback until they have learned this lesson. When a 1 understands the extent of their power, they will protect the weak, help the defenseless and accept responsibility where most others would avoid it. This power demands great courage as it mirrors the Heavenly Source of All Being, the very sacred energy that vibrates with the energy of the sun. 1 needs to be able to pull back and be him/herself, but must be careful when doing so not to end up becoming a recluse who believes that he/she does not need anybody. Being alone can easily develop into loneliness, and being unsociable can easily lead to being asocial.

When a I knows him/herself and understands his/ her responsibility and power, an immediate reaction to all action occurs, and life becomes a blissful river of gift upon gift. Helping, supporting and loving others, and being loved and respected, is just as important as the ability to freely draw breath.

SEED
I

You were among the chosen who stood on top of Mount Carmel, even before it was manifested in the physical world. You saw how everything on Earth was created in accordance with the etheric matrix of Truth, Love and Compassion provided by the Heavenly Source of All Being. You are forever carrying this knowledge of creation with you, being its supreme ambassador and initiator everywhere you go, and in everything you do. Now you have come here to create for the benefit of the common good and to support life in all its forms.

"The Holy and Mysterious One graved one point in a hidden recess. In that He enclosed the whole of creation as one who locks up his treasures in a place, under one key, which is therefore as valuable as all that is stored up in that place, for it is the key that shuts and opens."

(The Zohar, The Book of Light)

"The wind blows where it wishes, and you hear its sound, but you don't know where it comes from or where it goes. So is it with everyone who is born of the Spirit."   *(Gospel of John 3:8)*

"Let the seeker continue to seek until he finds. When he has found he will be worried. After worrying he will be astonished and will rule over everything."   *(Gospel of Thomas 2)*

"Show me the stone the builder has discarded. That one is the cornerstone."

(Gospel of Thomas 59)

"And this is the Father's will which has sent me, that of all which He has given me, I shall lose nothing, but shall raise it up again at the last day."

(Gospel of John 6:39)

Prayer for Aleph from Psalm 119:1-8:

¹ "Blessed are they whose ways are pure,
who walk in the path of the Light.
² Blessed are they who keep Its wisdom
and seek Its vibration with all their heart.
³ They radiate goodness;
they walk in the ways.
⁴ You contain the golden precepts
that I know in my mind and heart.
⁵ May my ways and words be steadfast
through living within Your Presence!
⁶ I thrive in abundance of gratitude
while I listen to Your guidance.
⁷ I AM the joy of my praise-filled heart
as I remember Your loving wisdom.
⁸ I merge with Your Light;
I AM One with You."

2

BEIT

ב

BLESSING AND DUALITY
The Magdalene

(B) (Prime) Water. Moon. The Archangel *Raziel*, "God's Secret". Dyad.

Kether – Binah	Will – Awareness
Gematria	2
Tarot	The High Priestess

Priestess. Divine Intuition. Duality. Balance. Growth. Partnership. Fertilizing, conception, birth and parenthood. The House of God.

PERSONALITY

Good imagination, dreams, intuition and sensitivity define this feminine principle. Number 2

47

desires peace and tolerance in all relationships and will try to please everyone if at all possible. A meticulous thinker who is not always able to put his/her thoughts into action, he/she can sometimes appear distant. A key challenge for 2 is to convert thoughts into practice and focus their energy on a particular project.

2 possesses a dreamy, idealistic and romantic nature, with energy that vibrates in the same way as that of the moon – fluctuating between extremes of emotion: sometimes incredibly open and loving, and at other times closed and fearful.

There is a great intuitive potential and high psychic energy. But 2s have to learn to develop sensitivity in order to be able to differentiate between illusion and reality. They often worry unnecessarily about loss and therefore easily feel that things are inadequate. This means that 2s need a stable base to come home to. Even when they go through terrible crises, a stable and secure home will protect them. For 2s, loss of their home will feel as if they have lost everything.

2s wouldn't cope well with travelling round the world, as they always need a safe haven. They therefore need to learn that "home" isn't necessarily a physical place, but an inner state – a state of belonging, security and connectedness.

Everything will go smoothly as long as 2s learn to focus and think positively. When they come to terms with fear and are able to maintain an inner calm, they will experience life opening up as if by magic and will realize that the universe is overflowing with all they have ever dreamt of.

SEED
2

You are the Wisdom, mentioned in Proverbs, which rejoiced in witnessing how everthing came to be. You are the sacred child of the Heavenly Source of All Being, Who chose you to represent Truth, Love and Compassion on Earth. You gave voice to the healing song of life and love, being the ambassador of sacred union in all relationships. Everything you do is done for the common good, revering life in all its forms. This is the widom you have come to share with your fellow human beings.

"I was sent forth from the Power, and I have come to those who reflect upon me, and I have been found among those who seek after me. Look upon me, you who reflect on me, and you hearers, hear me. (...) For I am the first and the last. I am the honored and the scorned one. I am the whore and the holy one. I am the wife and the virgin. I am the mother and the daughter. (...) I am the silence that is incomprehensible and the idea whose remembrance is frequent. I am the voice whose sound is manifold and the word whose appearance is multiple. I am the utterance of my name."

(*Thunder Perfect Mind*)

"I saw you there standing, trembling by the cross, you were the thunder and the lightning that ripped the veil apart, in the Holy of the Holies you were opening our hearts. I saw you there, holding that wounded bird in your hand, I saw the tears you were hiding, as you healed it by your command. It was not for Him you were crying, it was for us."

(*The Song of Mariam Mare*)

"Wisdom has built its palace with seven carved pillars." *(Book of Proverbs 9:1)*

"Wisdom (Sophia), which is regarded as being undefiled, is the mother of the angels; and the bride of Christ is Mariam the Magdalene. He loved Mariam more than the other disciples and often kissed her on the mouth." *(Gospel of Phillip 63:30-34)*

"I and my Bride are one, just as Mariam the Magdalene, whom I have chosen and dedicated to myself as an example, is one with me." *(Gospel of the Nazarenes 66:7-9)*

"And I will give unto you the keys of the Kingdom of Heaven, and whatsoever you shall loose on Earth shall be loosed in Heaven." *(Gospel of Matthew 16:19)*

Prayer for Beit from Psalm 119:9-16:

9 "How can I keep my ways pure?
By living according to Your love and vibration.
10 I feel Your Presence in my whole being;
let me remember Your guidance at all times.
11 I have placed Your word in my heart;
so I will always be close to You.
12 Praise and gratitude be to You;
I AM the merging of Your love and wisdom.
13 With my lips I recount
all the guidance that comes from Your mouth.
14 I rejoice in living in Your wisdom
as I feel its abundance of peace.
15 I meditate on Your precepts of Light
and consider Your glorious ways.
16 I delight in Your Presence;
I AM a fountain of Your word."

3

GIMEL

OPEN HEART & LOVING KINDNESS
The Queen of Sheba

(G) (Prime) Fire. Jupiter. The Archangel *Raguel*, "God's Friend". Triangle, triad. Proportion. Harmony. Wedding. Peace. The Universe. Friendship. Meaningfulness.

Kether –Tiphareth	Will – Grace
Gematria	3
Tarot	The Empress

Truth. Sincerity. Freedom. Generosity. Optimism. Movement. Expansion. Abundance. Birth of the Triumvirate. The Domain of Desire. Love. Beauty. Pleasure. 1-2-3-Go! Game. Impulsiveness.

Number 3 stands for growth and the necessity of having a foundation to stand on in order to reach a higher ideal. 3 is not content with anything less than the truth, be that in relationships between family, friends or at work. 3 can only find contentment when this goal has been reached. Some 3s reach their goal, while others delude themselves by believing in illusions.

3s deeply value independence, freedom of speech and everything else connected to freedom. Because they need flexibility and change, they can't commit themselves to lifelong agreements and obligations. They are instinctively aware that they can never be in possession of the whole truth so are always willing to learn and expand their understanding.

As 3s are always searching for the truth, they will either be a dedicated religious/spiritual person or a passionate atheist. It's one or the other. Religion can be an important part of their life, for, as soon as they have found their truth, they will dedicate themselves completely to this God, or Divine Energy that created the universe. 3s therefore often become priests or spiritual teachers. When 3s have searched and found, they exhibit great assurance, which will affect others and bring them peace and hope.

3s often need to move away from home or the workplace in order to feel completely free and alive. Sports, games and walking tours are some of the activities that can satisfy 3's need to stay active and in good shape.

A classic 3 will need to make sure that everything and everyone is okay. When they allow lack of judgment to decide a course of action, they can try to attribute the resulting mistakes to others. In doing so, they can sometimes go to extremes to prove their own infallibility. Never discuss with a 3. 3 has a tendency to use his or her energy up too quickly and therefore has to learn to conserve it. When 3 has learned to read life correctly, he or she makes a good leader, teacher or judge.

SEED
3

From the beginning of time you were shown how the physical universe is a most beautiful but still pale replica of the endless universe of true beauty within the human Soul. Travelling among the stars from universe to universe, you collected insights and wisdom from all forms of life, establishing within you the truth about the deeper meaning of love and how it is always available, wherever you are and whatever the circumstances. Now you go wherever you want by staying wherever you are – always projecting love and beauty. This is what you came here to teach and share with your fellow men.

"Do you believe because you have seen? Blessed the one who has believed without having seen."

(Gospel of John 20:29)

"The Kingdom of Heaven is like the leaven, which a woman took and buried in three measures of flour, until it was all leavened."

(Gospel of Matthew 13:33)

"The maiden is the daughter of Light. Upon her stands and rests the majestic effulgence of kings. Delightful is the sight of her, radiant with shining beauty. Her garments are like spring flowers, and a scent of sweet fragrance is diffused from them. In the crown of her head the king is established, feeding with his own ambrosia those who are set under him. Truth rests upon her head. By the movement of her feet she shows forth joy. Her mouth is open, because she sings loud songs of praise. Thirty and two are they that sing her praises. Her two hands make signs and secret patterns, proclaiming the dance of the blessed Aeons. Her fingers open the gates of the city. Her chamber is full of Light, breathing a scent of balsam and all sweet herbs, and giving out a sweet smell of myrrh and aromatic leaves. The Father of Truth and the Mother of Wisdom are always with her."

(*Acts of Thomas*)

"I am, therefore, ready to accept God's will. Let it happen as You have said."

(*Gospel of Luke 1:38*)

Prayer for Gimel from Psalm 119:17-24:

17 "May the vibration of grace fill me;
may love guide every step I make.
18 Open my eyes, that I may see
wonderful things in Your Presence.
19 I have chosen to come to Earth;
I AM the revelation of my being and purpose.
20 My soul is radiating my love and longing
for Your Light at all times.
21 You reach out to the arrogant, who are lost
and who forgot Your Presence and guidance.
22 I AM the transformation of all shadows,
in me and around me, for I AM Light.
23 If rulers sit together in ignorance,
I AM the merging with Your love.
24 Your Presence is my delight;
It is my guide and my home."

4

19

DALETH

ד

DIMENSIONS & PRESENCE
King Solomon

(D) Earth. Uranus. The Door. The Archangel *Ramiel*, "God's Mercy". Transformation. Justice.

Hochmah – Binah	Wisdom – Awareness
Gematria	4
Tarot	The Emperor

Centered toward the Infinite Point. Architecture of Power. Stability. Individuality. Ingenuity. Tolerance. Shield. Transformation. Forgiveness. The Unexpected. The Four Elements. The Four Corners of the World. Simple and natural lifestyle. Tao.

This number stands for stability – 4 is grounded and independent, balanced and at peace with him/herself. 4 is tolerant of others and of anything unfamiliar. 4 tries to share his/her own inner peace and stability with everyone else, too, and is therefore very inspiring.

4 is seldom understood by others and is somewhat of a mystery, so is hard to predict or second-guess. 4 is in harmony with Uranus, which leads to unexpected changes. And 4 makes his/her own rules which means that his/her actions and words can shock others.

4 foresees the future and is often the first to try something new. 4 therefore has a tendency to ignore those who can't keep up.

4 doesn't interfere in other people's lives and believes that everyone should learn from their own mistakes, sometimes causing him/her to overlook others. When 4 is not in balance, he/she can take on other people's burdens.

4 doesn't see any reason to repair anything that isn't broken and is content with simplicity. 4's motto is "Live and let live". 4 is just as happy with a tent in the desert as a house in the city.

SEED
4

You were among the builders of the physical world. You were the balancing power that had to take responsibility when no one else had the courage. Through hard-earned experience you saw how easily cruelty manifests in those nowhere-places where the consciousness of Light is being rejected. You are the power of the Heavenly Source of All Being. You went into the dark and cleared the way for Truth, Love and Compassion. You manifest and serve the Infinite Point in the hearts of your fellow men by your very being.

"Healing will descend in dew, disease will withdraw, and worry and pain and lamentation will be unknown to men, and felicity will cover the Earth. No one will die untimely nor will adversity strike. Judgments, reviling, contention, revenge, blood, passion, envy, hatred will all be condemned and removed. For those are the evils that fill the world and trouble man. Wild beasts will leave the forest and minister to men, and asps and dragons will come out of their holes and serve a little child. For in that time the corruptible will vanish and the incorruptible will have its beginning, to which good things belong, far from evil and near the immortal. This is the bright lightning that came after the last dark waters."

(*The Angel Ramiel in The Apocalypse of Baruch*)

"Blessed the one who comes in the name of the Lord!" (*Gospel of Luke 19:38*)

"Only the one who understands how to serve, can rule." (*Yeshua*)

"These things have I spoken unto you that in me you might have peace. In the world you shall experience tribulation, but be of good cheer for I have overcome the world."

(*Gospel of John 16:33*)

"And have you not read the scripture, the stone which the builders rejected has become the cornerstone." *(Gospel of Mark 12:10)*

Prayer for Daleth from Psalm 119:25-32:

25 "I raise all worldly matters into Your Presence;
fill my life with Your vibration.
26 I recounted my ways and You answered me;
guide me to see and share Your blessings.
27 Let me realize the vastness of Your wisdom
as I meditate on Your wonders.
28 When I walk the path of pain and sorrow,
comfort and strengthen me in Your Light.
29 I AM the truth, the way and the life;
the grace of Your Presence is with me always.
30 I have chosen the way of truth;
my heart is filled with Your Light.
31 I hold fast to Your vibration;
I will never lose my way.
32 I AM the path of Your love,
for Your Presence has set my heart free."

5

18

HEH

ה

DIVINITY & ILLUMINATION
Melchizedek

(H) (Prime) Air. Mercury. The Archangel *Sariel*, "God is my Prince". Illumination in Solitude. Hermes. Close to the Heavenly Source of all Being. Priest-King. The Initiator. Inner Guide. Teacher. The Five Senses. Isogenic. Light. Here Am I. The Pentagon.

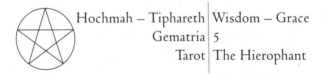

Hochmah – Tiphareth	Wisdom – Grace
Gematria	5
Tarot	The Hierophant

Intellect. Patience. Communication. Movement. Versatility. Adaptability. Entrepreneurialism. Comfort. Freedom.

The number 5 has good manners and great charm, which is often used to gain the respect of, or to satisfy, others. In this way, 5 is easily able to communicate his or her thoughts and ideas to others.

5 can have a tendency to perfectionism and is quick to notice their own and others' mistakes.

5 needs change and movement in order to compensate for the lack of any perfect answer. 5 can have difficulties with relationships, because he or she is always trying to understand why they love the other or why the other loves them. Instead, it would be good if 5 could learn to accept that love is not an intellectual exercise, but a feeling and an expression that flows from the heart.

5 can be pedantic and is probably the only person who reads the small print on the back of a packet of oats or the official announcements in a newspaper.

5 requires freedom, but in order to gain it can sometimes hamper the freedom of others. 5 loves comfort, is good at coping in all situations and is incredibly sociable.

SEED
5

You are after the Order of Melchizedek forever, supporting the line of incarnations of Messiahs, Avatars and Bodhisattvas, and being a teacher and helper of the I AM yourself. You drew the circle and sat there for an eternity, until the alchemy of the Heavenly Source of All Being was done and you had become pure Light. You were shown the necessity of solitude and silence in developing true illumination, and through your experiences you have come to show your fellow human beings how it can be done — forever serving the Order of Melchizedek.

"Expand yourself to the same extent as the immeasurable Greatness; leap out of all body, and transcend all time; become Eternity, and you shall perceive the Heavenly Source of All Being. Realize that to you nothing is impossible; believe yourself to be immortal and able to grasp all things — every art, every science, and the way of life of every living creature. Become higher than all height and lower than all depth; gather in yourself all the feelings of the created, of fire, of water, dry and wet. Perceive that you are everywhere at the same time — on earth, at sea, in heaven; not yet born, in the womb, young, old, just dead, in the after-death. Having perceived all these at once — times, places, facts, qualities — then you can perceive the Heavenly Source of All Being. But if you imprison your Soul in the body and insult it, saying, 'I know nothing, can do nothing; I fear the sea, I am unable to climb into the sky; I know not who I was, nor do I know who I shall be' — then what have you to do with the Heavenly Source of All Being?"

(Corpus Hermetica)

"The Eye through which I see God is the same through which God sees me. My Eye and God's Eye are one and the same in seeing, one and the same in knowing, one and the same in loving."

(Meister Eckhart)

"And Melchizedek, Jerusalem's King, priest of the most high God, came toward him. He brought bread and wine."

(Book of Genesis 14:18)

"Such is it ordained: You belong to the Melchizedek order forever."

(Letter to the Hebrews 7:17)

"Teaching them to observe all things whatsoever I have taught you; and lo, I AM with you always, even to the end of the world."

(Gospel of Matthew 28:20)

"Blessed are your eyes for they see; and your ears for they hear."

(Gospel of Matthew 13:16)

Prayer for Heh from Psalm 119:33-40:

33 "Fill me with Your Light;
I will share it forever.
34 I AM the understanding of Your wisdom;
my heart remembers all Your sacred seeds.
35 Open my path to Your Presence,
for there I AM delight.
36 Turn my heart toward Your vibration;
let me overflow with love to all beings.
37 Turn my eyes toward worthy causes;
hold my life in the power of Your word.
38 I AM the fulfillment of all that is needed;
my life is the open door to You.
39 Transform all disharmony;
I AM the vibration of grace.
40 How I delight in Your Presence!
I AM the guidance of the Light."

6

VAV

ו

COMPLETION & TRANSFORMATION
The Bridal Chamber

(V, W) (Perfect) Water. Venus. The Archangel *Raphael*, "The Angel of Healing". The Hexagon. Peace. The one who joins two separates together. Love and Compassion. Eros. Serpent. Apple. Wisdom. Harmony in Opposition. The merging of the Masculine and the Feminine. The Archetype of Service. The form of forms. Cosmos. All-healing. The whole.

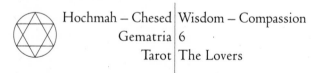

	Hochmah – Chesed	Wisdom – Compassion
	Gematria	6
	Tarot	The Lovers

Magnetic attraction. Introverted, but sociable. A romantic. The Archetype of Service.

The number 6 stands for the feminine essence within compassion and love. 6 is universally well-liked, possesses a particular charisma and radiates and attracts love. 6 is born romantic and can be correspondingly sentimental.

6 is also of a practical nature: he/she sees what needs to be done and does it. 6 hates conflict and loves to foster peace when there are differences. Jealousy and bitterness can tear 6's heart apart. This is why 6 will always try to find the solution to a problem. Although introverted, 6 is sociable and possesses a large circle of friends, which includes people from all social strata.

Money and success always follow 6. A situation of want only develops if 6 thinks negatively or becomes depressed. 6 only has him/herself to blame if things don't go as they wish, although they will often try to find the cause of the problem elsewhere.

As long as 6 understands that he/she is here to be sociable, show love and allow a stream of loving, life-giving energy to flow freely, they will be surrounded by happiness and success. 6's magnetic disposition will attract more goodness and happiness. 6's key words are: compassion, love and social responsibility.

SEED
6

First there was one, then there were two. Then the merging. When the separation arrived You were called in from the stars to mend the broken, raise the fallen and heal the sick. From the very beginning of time you were shown the Bridal Chamber with its healing powers. You know how the joining of separate forces can only happen through the alchemy of love and compassion on all levels. There can never be any separation between love-making and love. You have come to share the fact that there can never be any truth without love. Everything but love is an illusion.

"She took hold of him and kissed him and brazenly told him that she had just brought the Lord a gift: 'I have given myself today, therefore, I have come to meet you and be close to you and I have found you!'"

(*Book of Proverbs 7:13-15*)

"The one who becomes a child of the Bridal Chamber will receive the Light. The one who does not receive it there will not be able to receive it elsewhere. The one who has received the Light cannot be seen or restrained and no one in this world will be able to hurt her. Furthermore, when she leaves this world, she will already have received the truth in images."

(Gospel of Phillip 127)

"I, Wisdom, repose in fidelity and I have insight and discretion. I love those who love me, and those who search for me, find me."

(Book of Proverbs 7:12&17)

"I and my bride are one, just as Mariam the Magdalene, whom I have chosen and dedicated to myself as an example, is one with me."

(Gospel of the Nazarenes 66:7-9)

"And as a new commandment I give unto you, that you love one another as I have loved you."

(Gospel of John 13:34)

"Let me be the seal upon your heart and the ring upon your finger; because love is stronger than death. Its outbreak is like a blazing fire, a flame of Eternity." *(Song of Songs 8:6-7)*

Prayer for Vav from Psalm 119:41-48:

41 "I AM love,
the vibration of Your Presence.
42 From here I will answer all calls,
the caring and the taunting ones.
43 The words I speak are words of truth,
while I rest in Your peace and guidance.
44 I AM the fulfillment of Your Light,
for ever and ever.
45 I walk and talk in freedom,
for I AM One with You.
46 I will speak of Your Presence before kings
and will find the way to their hearts,
47 for I am held in Your Light
and carried by It throughout eternity.
48 I open my arms to Your embrace
and give myself with all my love."

7

ZAYIN

ז

SPIRIT & MYSTERY
The Chariot of Fire

(Z) (Prime) Air. Neptune. The Archangel *Uriel*, "The Fire of God". The Heptagon. Aiming for Heaven. Spiritually Gifted. The Light that shines through the Universe. Facing the Wind. Destiny.

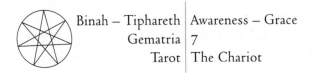

Binah – Tiphareth	Awareness – Grace
Gematria	7
Tarot	The Chariot

Wisdom. Spirituality. Sensitivity. Mystery. Counseling skills. All cycles built upon the holy number 7.

PERSONALITY

The number 7 stands for the supernatural and the inexplicable – the deepest mysteries of life. 7 represents faith and healing, but can also conceal illusions and unrealistic dreams. 7 can easily become dependent on other people, other things, inappropriate behavior or stimulants.

7s always get what they need, rather than what they desire. They have a relaxed attitude to work and money, because they don't feel they receive more than the minimum payment for their efforts.

7s possess great intuitive insight, can be clairvoyant and are able to express themselves artistically. A 7's spiritual freedom gives him/her access to the creative force and deep intuition necessary to make them a very good counselor. Being self-sufficient, 7 is good at working alone.

SEED
7

You were the first star in the heavens. You were put there as a guiding Light for the lost and the lonely. From this Light seven rays of Truth, Healing, Wisdom, Beauty, Joy, Love and Compassion were projected and sent down, hovering over the Earth. Now you have incarnated here to clear the sky of the clouds of ignorance, showing your fellow human beings the seven rays of this Sacred Light. It is on the beams of the Sacred Light of the Seven Attributes that you shall return to the highest levels in your Chariot of Fire.

"I have come because my Father sent me, but you will not listen to me. However, there are those who were not sent by the Father and who recommend themselves to you to whom you are very willing to listen."

(*Gospel of John 5:43*)

Yeshua said:

"If they say to you, 'Where did you come from?' – say to them, 'We came from the Light, the place where the Light came into being on its own accord and established itself and became manifest through their image.' If they say to you, 'Is it you?' – say, 'We are its children, and we are the elect of the Living Father.' If they ask you, 'What is the sign of the Living Father?' – say to them, 'It is movement and rest.'"

(Gospel of Thomas, logion 50)

"Then the devil left Him and angels came and took care of Him."

(Gospel of Matthew 4:11)

"Because this is the secret: If your faith is like a mustard seed, you will be able to move mountains and nothing will be impossible for you."

(Gospel of Matthew 19:20)

Prayer for Zayin from Psalm 119:49-56

49 "I AM the Presence of Your word,
in which my being radiates like a sun.
50 I AM the comfort of Your Light,
in which my life meets suffering or joy.
51 If the arrogant try to mock and restrain,
I enter into the Presence of Your love.
52 I remember Your eternal wisdom,
and I surrender to its grace.
53 I AM compassion for the wicked,
who have forgotten Your Presence.
54 Your vibration is the theme of my song
wherever I AM, whatever I do.
55 In the night I remember Your name;
I AM the keeper of Your Light.
56 This is my being and my practice:
I AM love, forevermore."

8

CHET

TRANSCENDENCE & DIVINE GRACE
Integrity

Earth. Saturn. The Archangel *Mikael*, "He who is similar to God." The Octagon. Throne. The Dominion of Grace.

	Binah — Gevurah	Awareness — Truth	
	Gematria	8	
	Tarot	Justice	

Steadfastness. Parent. Harmony. Wisdom. Patience. Security. Shield. Charity. Self-control. King. Leader. Warrior. Loyalty. Lifeline. Eternity. Infinity.

8's wisdom and stability emanates from his/her own hard work and experience, which wins great respect from others. 8 is in contact with the stable planet Saturn, which moves slowly and beautifully along its own path around the sun.

8's self-discipline and engagement often results in reaching a goal that others haven't managed to attain, have given up on, or have never even considered. 8 is usually shy, quiet and reserved and seldom shows his/her true self. 8 is often the victim of other peoples' cunning, cheating or deception, because they appear naive and gullible. However, 8s actually have unusually strong personalities and don't easily forget those who have hurt them.

The quality of patience makes 8 an exemplary teacher. Any task or profession that requires determination, endurance and patience will be perfect for an 8. They would make good mountain climbers, as any goal they set themselves is usually reached at some point.

8 is the holy number that rules over karma and reincarnation, death and rebirth. An 8 therefore often feels as if he/she has been sent to earth with a particular task. 8 doesn't take things lightly. Everything has a purpose. Nothing is meaningless.

As 8 grows older and achieves his/her ambitions, they feel correspondingly younger. 8 often behaves in a more youthful way as a 50 year-old than they did as a 20 year-old.

SEED
8

Before the beginning of time you were shown the Fountain of Everlasting Life, with its generating and healing powers. You saw that death is just a portal between the worlds, that there is only one life, which is eternal. You have seen and experienced everything in the world. Through these experiences you came to understand the purpose of relation-ships and their deep effect on building and transforming karma. Through this you were given the integrity of the Heavenly Source of All Being. This is the gift you came here to share with the world.

"He who would gain a golden understanding of the word *truth*, should have the eyes of his Soul opened, and his mind illumined by the inward Light which the Heavenly Source of All Being has kindled in our hearts from the beginning. Although no man ever has, or ever can, see the Heavenly Source of All Being with his outward bodily eyes, yet with the inward eyes of the Soul It may well be seen and known."

(The Sophic Hydrolith)

"The time will come when time is meaningless and place is nowhere. All our concepts wait but their appointed ending. They uphold a dream with no dimensions. At the gate of Heaven are they merely laid aside before the blazing of the Light within."

(Helen Schucman)

"The one who judges others, judges himself."

(Yeshua)

"The inner room of practice is always with you. You can practice everywhere, in the church and in the supermarket, in the meditation room and in the concert hall, in a back alley and on the high street. It is only a matter of being present and remembering, whatever the circumstances. Whatever you say to your loved ones or strangers in public must be measured by the thoughts you have and the deeds you do when you are without witnesses. When you are able to *be* what you preach or project, you have attained true integrity. When this is achieved, you start to experience the workings of Divine Grace. It will be with you everywhere you go, blessing everything you do."

(Lamu)

"Wisdom is with You, she knows Your works, she was with You when You created the world; she knows what You are working toward and the goal of Your highest command."

(Book of Wisdom 9:9)

57 "You are my will and my way,
I remember Your words in the depth of my soul.
58 I AM Your Presence within my heart;
Your grace and blessings are with me always.
59 On every path, every day,
I turn my eyes and steps to Your Light.
60 I AM the fulfillment
of Your wisdom.
61 If the wicked bind me with ropes,
I AM the power and might of everlasting love.
62 In the midst of the night
I AM the Light of eternal gratitude.
63 I am a friend to all who have forgotten,
and to all who remember their garments of truth.
64 The Earth is filled with Your love;
I AM the Light of the world."

9

TETH

ט

COMPLETION & WISDOM
In the Desert, The Unprotected

(T) Air. Mars. The Archangel *Gabriel*, "The Voice of God", "The Angel of Annunciation". Ouroboros. A Solitary Light. Enneade. Helios. Bridge. Passage. Companion. Perfection.

Chesed – Gevurah	Compassion – Truth
Gematria	9
Tarot	The Hermit

If the Unprotected is *conscious*: striving to make him/herself a channel for God-Consciousness through purification and meditation. If *unconscious*: open to all kinds of trials and tests. Action, courage and conflict. Lovable and sociable. Focused, original, a seeker of wholeness. Honesty. The completion of a cycle and the beginning of a new one.

PERSONALITY

The number 9 is connected to the power of action, and usually gets what he or she wants. 9 sets processes in motion and is a catalyst for movement. 9 makes quick decisions, often without a backward glance. 9 can, at times, be too quick off the mark, and in such cases finds it difficult to take responsibility for a mistake. "What you see is what you get" is 9's attitude.

9's obstinacy often prevents attainment of the higher aim. He/she doesn't allow anything to distract them from moving toward the intended goal and can easily be too superficial. On the other hand, if 9 is aware and manages to overcome that obstinacy and superficiality, he/she will experience a free flow of spirituality, and life will become the gift that they have always dreamed of.

9 is involved in the great cycle. He/she is therefore good at assessing wholeness and often leaves the minor details to others. This is true both of practical relations at work and in matters of the heart and personal relationships. When

9 acknowledges his/her true potential and doesn't get lost in unnecessary detail, they are original thinkers — autonomous individuals who do away with the old and lead others toward the new.

SEED
9

You were the first who stepped down from Mount Carmel and went into the desert to rid yourself of all the noise created by fear and uncertainty. This was the beginning that has no end. You paved the way for the Messiah by showing those who came after you how the freedom of choice that every human being is given must be held in the highest regard. You were taken to the end of time and shown both the sea of grace and the abyss of hopelessness. There, you understood that giving up in despair is not an option. Then you raised your hands and gave it Up and left it into the care of the Heavenly Source of All Being. This is the gift you came to share with the world.

"One of the challenges man has to face is that whatever he engages himself in, it will always, one day, come to an end. Everything in the physical realm has its appointed time. This also goes for the incarnated human being. The only thing he can be sure of when incarnating is that someday he will leave again. A lifetime is a long line of hellos and goodbyes. Yet he will have to learn the lesson that he is a spiritual being who, although right now residing in a physical body, is in truth always boundlessly free and can go wherever he wants. When he realizes that he can transform all his worries and fears by dedicating himself wholeheartedly to the Heavenly Source of All Being, he himself will be a haven of peace and calm, hope and healing to his fellow men."

(*Lamu*)

"My brother, the brave man has to give his life away. Give it, I advise thee; — thou dost not expect to sell thy life in an adequate manner? Give it, like a royal heart; let the price be nothing: thou hast then, in a certain sense, got All for it! The heroic man — and is not every man, God be thanked, a potential hero? — has to do so, in all times and circumstances." (*Thomas Carlyle*)

"Narrow the gate and strait the path, that leads
to life. Only a few discover it."

(*Gospel of Matthew 7:14*)

Prayer for Teth from Psalm 119:65-72:

65 "I AM the radiance of Your Light
as I walk my path in Your Presence.
66 I AM the wisdom of grace
that leads my heart and hands.
67 If I ever forget, in pain or sorrow,
I AM the return to Your guiding Light.
68 Your peace bears unspeakable goodness;
I share it wherever I go.
69 If the arrogant are lying and smearing,
my answers are guided by caring.
70 Their hearts are lonely and cold,
while I feel the embrace of Your love.
71 I cherish all my choices, whatever they brought,
for they lead me to know myself.
72 I AM the Presence of Your wisdom,
the abundance of Your precious Light."

10

13

YOD

׳

THE INFINITE POINT
The Book of Life

(Y, I, J) "God's Hand". Keeper of the Keys. Messenger. Decade. Eternity. Strong Intuition. Necessity. Destiny. Cycles of the Elements. Memory. Heaven. Charity.

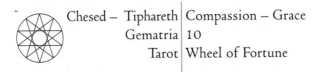

Chesed – Tiphareth	Compassion – Grace
Gematria	10
Tarot	Wheel of Fortune

The number of Sefirot on the kabbalistic Tree of Life (see p.172). The Number of Destiny. No middle road. Either/or. Black/white. Love/hate. To read between the lines. The one who turns the pages. Receives with one hand in Heaven and delivers with the other what is needed on Earth.

Yod is the smallest of all the letters and is the first letter in the name of Yeshua and YHWH.

The number 10 always tries to take things to the next level. In the process, a 10 can be impatient and move too fast, thereby missing the true purpose of moving. 10 carries all the qualities of a great leader and visionary. Only if they neglect their intuitive abilities will they stagnate and lose their grip on true leadership. 10 is the number of fulfillment.

SEED
10

You are one of the scribes who dedicated your service to the Heavenly Source of All Being and Its creation of everything. You were among those who recorded the frequencies of all conscious experiences from all created beings in all universes. Every time a pen is touching the membrane of time, the beginning of a story and a destiny is being written, read and experienced simultaneously. You are the Keeper of the Keys to the Book of Life. You are one of its scribes and its translators, who has come here to share its secrets with your fellow human beings.

"Isis: 'Be aware, O my son Horus; for you will be introduced to the secret teaching that Kaemphis the Elder first taught. It was he who introduced Hermes (Messiah) to that teaching, Kaemphis, the oldest amongst our people. I heard it from Hermes, he who writes everything in the Book of Life, when he initiated me in the ritual of perfection.'"

(Hermes Trismegistus)

"Blessed are those who regret their mistakes, they shall be healed of their mental pain."

(Gospel of Matthew 5:4)

"All creatures are with God: The being that they have God gives them with His presence. The bride in the Book of Love said: 'I have run round the circle and have found no end to it, so I cast myself into the centre.' This circle, which the loving Soul ran round, is all the Trinity has ever wrought. Spent with her quest, she casts herself into the centre. This point of the Trinity wherein unmoved it is doing all its work. Therein the Soul becomes omnipotent."

(Meister Eckhart)

"It is written: Man shall not live by bread alone, but by each and every word coming from God Himself."

(Gospel of Matthew 4:7)

Prayer for Yod from Psalm 119:73-80:

73 "Your vibration is my home;
I AM Your wisdom and Your love.
74 May those who forgot You rejoice when they
see me, for I AM the emanation of Your Light.
75 I remember the reality of Your Presence;
even in hardship I feel Your love and guidance.
76 I AM boundless love and endless comfort
as I embrace Your eternal might and power.
77 I AM the compassion that I seek,
and I live in the delight of Your word.
78 May the hearts of the arrogant be opened,
no matter what was said or done,
as I AM the constant stream of Your Light.
79 May those who deny You turn to me,
those who have forgotten Your Presence.
80 May my heart be radiating Your essence;
I AM the fulfillment of my quest and being."

I I

KAPH

OMNIPRESENCE & VISION
The Cup of Destiny, The Seer

Master number. (K, C) (Prime) Clear Psychic Vision.
The Third Eye. Action and Consequence.

Chesed – Netzach	Compassion – Victory
Gematria	20
Tarot	Strength

PERSONALITY

I I is the most intuitive of all the numbers. It
represents Enlightenment; a channel to the subconscious, insight released from rational thought.

11 is sensitive and shy, has nervous energy, and can appear impractical. 11 is a dreamer. 11 has all of 2's aspects, but to a greater extent and full of charisma, leadership and inspiration. The number possesses an inbuilt duality that creates dynamism, but also inner conflict.

11 is a number that can easily become too introverted and can create fears and phobias if he or she doesn't keep focused on the goal and steer away from the little self, the ego. This means 11 balances on a thin line between rise and fall. Which side of the line he or she ends up on is completely up to them.

11's potential for growth, stability and personal strength lies solely in the acceptance of his or her powers of intuition and unless this is acknowledged and used, intuition won't make use of 11.

11 has to learn to trust and nurture his or her belief in, and understanding of, spiritual truths. 11 won't find peace in logic, but in faith.

11 is clairvoyant and is always working toward 22.

Coming down from Mount Carmel, you were left in the desert. Then after forty days you were surrounded by the beasts of your own making and shown your destiny, crucified on the cross of time and space. You prayed for mercy and were given the Cup of Resurrection. You took it and drank its everlasting truth, which made you able to see through all illusions and read between the lines of life in whatever form it appears. In that moment you understood what a human being is and why it was created. Now you have come to share your experience with those who have ears to hear and eyes to see.

"The Angel answered: 'The Holy Spirit will come upon you and His power will work wonders within you. Therefore, the holy child you will bear will be called the Son of God.'"

(Gospel of Luke 1:35)

"And I asked the angel that took me and initiated me in the secret knowledge of the Son of Man who He was and why He was with the Ancient of Days? And the angel answered me: 'This is the Son of Man, He who is just and with whom justice rests, He who uncovers the hidden and heavenly insights. The Lord of the Spirits has chosen Him, for the Son of Man has existed since before the dawn of time and will be the blessing of the Lord of the Spirits forever.'"

(1st Book of Enoch 46:2-3)

"In the Ark of the Covenant, above the place of reconciliation between the cherubs, I will meet you and talk to you and give you all the commands that concern my people of Israel."

(Book of Exodus 25:22)

"For in Christ the whole of God's being is revealed in human form, and you can receive all you need from Him."

(Letter to the Colossians 2:9)

"Lord, let this cup pass from me! Yet not my will, but Thy will be done."

(Gospel of Luke 22:42)

Prayer for Kaph from Psalm 119:81-88:

81 "My soul sings with gratitude and longing;
I AM the peace beyond all understanding.
82 I close my eyes and open my hands,
receiving Your Presence in my heart.
83 If I ever doubt my doing or being,
I AM the return of Your Light.
84 I AM the blessing of patience;
my compassion and love always flourish!
85 If the arrogant dig pitfalls for me,
I meet them in Your Presence.
86 I AM Your Light and Your wisdom;
Your guidance shows me words and ways.
87 No matter who or what I face on Earth,
I AM the Oneness of all Heavens.
88 Your love fills my life, my heart, my soul,
I AM the Light of Your word."

12

II

LAMED

ל

EXAMPLE & PURPOSE
Crucifixion

(L) Death of The Ego. Ego-Free. The Space Between. The Universal Spirit. Healer and Teacher.

Gevurah – Tiphareth	Truth – Grace
Gematria	30
Tarot	The Hanged Man

PERSONALITY

12 is the number of dedication and change – to dedicate oneself to others or be an easy victim for the intrigue of others. 12s must learn not

to take on other people's burdens with the purpose of receiving redemption for themselves, yet they will be freed from pain by taking on the pain of others who suffer. This is the ultimate trust and faith in God and the Universe and will lead you to the next step of transformation: *Transfiguration*.

SEED
12

You were given the choice to experience purification through the crucifixion of the ego, or the "little self". You went through the humiliation of losing everything and at the same time being scorned and laughed at. In this way, you understood the impermanence of everything that is not upheld by Truth, Love and Compassion. Now you have come to share your experience with the world. Only what is eternal does not pass away. Everything else is like fleeting ghosts with no substance.

"The ego is a tricky companion who thrives by doing 'good deeds', charity work and the like – as long as it gets something in return. It insists on getting other people's recognition for the good deeds it has performed. We live in a world where many of us are focusing more on the external image of their personality than the inner image of the Heavenly Source of All Being in which they were created. It is a form of narcissism that can only be healed through spiritual work, practicing genuine generosity. Be anonymous when you give. See what is needed – apply it – then leave, being content that the rest will be taken care of. This is the only way to heal the world, because the White Dove of Divine Grace ascends everywhere genuine generosity and healing is being practiced."

(*Lamu*)

"Then Yeshua said: 'I say unto you: Only when a person is born again can he or she enter the Kingdom of God. One must be born of both water and spirit before one can enter the Kingdom of Heaven.'"

(*Gospel of John 3:3 & 5*)

"Father, into Your hands I commit my spirit."
(*Gospel of Luke 23:46*)

Prayer for Lamed from Psalm 119:89-96:

89 "Your word and wisdom are eternal;
their power reaches from Heaven to Earth.
90 I AM the faith passed on by the mighty Ones;
the ancient glory of the Earth rejoices
in all her splendor.
91 Now and forever, Your Light fills all existence
and all things radiate Your Presence.
92 I AM the delight in Your wisdom,
it comforts and strengthens me at all times.
93 I AM the remembrance of Your love;
it is the sacred breath of my life.
94 Your Presence is my belonging and my safety;
I AM Your guidance.
95 If I face wickedness or destruction,
I open Your shield of peace.
96 Whatever my eyes or ears perceive,
I AM merging with Your boundless Light."

13

MEM

מ

THE CONCEALED & THE REVEALED
Transfiguration

(M) (Prime) The Concealed is being Revealed.
The Inside-Out State of Being. From Atonement to
At-One-Ment. Catharsis. Transformation. Change.

Gevurah – Hod	Truth – Presence
Gematria	40
Tarot	Death

PERSONALITY

The number 13 stands for perfection and transformation. Known as the Christ number, it is one
of the holiest and most blessed of numbers, which
means it attracts good fortune and new life.

You were shown the space between the worlds, and the etheric Light on the other side of the veil. You saw the Sacred SHM Seed of the Heavenly Source of All Being, and the Light that emanates from this seed. Being aware that all human beings are carrying the Sacred Seed within. and how it is being nurtured and opened, you brought this knowledge of the Light into the world. You saw the Light from the Transfiguration of Yeshua the Messiah when he showed himself on the mountain as he really is, so it might be known among the living and the dead, that there is no dying nor death. The physical proof of this Light is to be seen on the Shroud of Turin. Now you have come to show that Transfiguration is the image of what has always been and what will always be: Truth, Love and Compassion.

"In as much as you bring to light that which is within you, it will redeem you. In as much as you do not bring to light that which is within you, it will destroy you."

(Gospel of Thomas, logion 70)

"I Am Transfiguration
A leaf blown by the wind
There never was a beginning
And there'll never be an end."

(The God Formula)

"Transfiguration is the very presence of the highest qualities, the Divine Nature and Heritage, that humans can aspire to in the physical incarnation. Yeshua showed his transfigured being, his etheric Lightbody to some of the disciples in order to have them understand the implications and the deep connection to man's core being or Sacred Seed within, which must be the center and foundation of all thoughts, words and deeds in our lives. To become One with our Divine Nature."

(Lamu)

"The Eye is the Light of the body, therefore, when your Eye is opened your whole being will be filled with Light."

(Gospel of Matthew 6:22-23)

Prayer for Mem from Psalm 119:97-104:

97 "Oh, how I love Your Light!
It fills my being day and night.
98 Your guidance is always with me;
I AM the purity of Your wisdom.
99 I AM the insight of Your essence
when I meditate on Your love.
100 I extend the blessings of the Ancient Ones,
as I merge with Your guiding Light.
101 My feet walk on sacred ground;
I AM Your word and Your way.
102 Your Light embraces me forever,
Your very Presence directs my path.
103 How sweet is the advent of Your vibration,
with all senses I receive Your love!
104 My heart unfolds Your wisdom
while I bless every step of our way."

14

NUN

נ

FIDELITY & SOUL
Guardian Angel

(N) Invisible Protective Force. Center of the Storm. Counselor. Charity. Purity.

Tiphareth – Netzah	Grace – Victory
Gematria	50
Tarot	Temperance

PERSONALITY

14 means continuity through change, movement and communication, adaptability in all situations and personal relationships, and great intuitive ability.

You were raised among the Angels who showed you the very essence of life, the golden Substance of Love, of which a small seed is planted in every created being. In this substance you found the care, charity and compassion given to all guardian angels to distribute among the living and to fill every heart and empty space with their healing power of loving kindness. The Guardian Angel is applying its gifts without making a fuss about it. It is purifying the world and everyone in it with its invisible presence. Now you have come to bear witness to the work of the Guardian Angel within.

"I am Gabriel who stands before God's face, and I am sent to talk to you and bring you this joyful message."

(Gospel of Luke 1:19)

"All who drink of the worldly water will thirst once more; but those who drink of the water I have access to will never thirst again. This water will be a life-giving source within man, which will lead to eternal life."

(Gospel of John 4:13-14)

Prayer for Nun from Psalm 119:105-112:

105 "Your word is a lamp to my feet
and a light on my path.
106 I dedicate myself
to live Your love.
107 I place the suffering of my past
into the flames of Your hand.
108 I AM the acceptance of Your praise;
now I will always sing its song.
109 When I move through my everydays,
Your grace and glory guide my way.
110 Whatever was, whatever will be,
I AM the mighty rock of Your Presence.
111 Your Light is my eternal heritage;
It is the joy of my heart and soul.
112 My heart is set on keeping
Your wisdom and love forevermore."

15

SAMECH

PROTECTION & MEMORY
The Shadow

(S) Passion. Transcending Limitation. Breaking through and becoming whole. Grounding.

Tiphareth – Yesod	Grace – Foundation
Gematria	60
Tarot	The Devil

PERSONALITY

The number 15 represents magic, mystery and being endowed with peace, unconditional love and good fortune. 15 thrives when they are together with others, because they pass on goodness and happiness to everyone they meet.

SEED
15

After man was given free will, the Shadow was born. You were with Yeshua in the cave at Qumran when he spent his 40 days in the desert. You witnessed the wild beasts gathering around him, until he realized that they were shadows of his own making. In the end you saw how Yeshua had to face his own ego, which was showing itself in the guise of Satan. Now you have come to reveal how this process is the very last initiation that must be taken before man can know true freedom — the freedom to genuinely share his gift with the world.

"External life is the shadow of the inner reality."
(Hazrat Inayat Khan)

"It is not so strange, because Satan himself claims to be one of the angels of Light."
(2nd letter to the Corinthians 11:14)

"Man has only one self. But it consists of two sides, one called ego or the little self and the other the divine or higher Self. Which one is in play is determined by the choices we are making. Way too often we are allowing the little self to play its dramas without paying attention to its destructive nature, directed from our subconscious mind. Most of us step back from facing this dark side of our being without knowing that, by inviting it out into the Light, we would find the most precious gifts hidden among the traumas that just await our invitation to be transformed."

(Lamu)

"When you stand with your back to the sun, your shadow is before you; but when you turn and face the sun, then your shadow falls behind you."

(Hazrat Inayat Khan)

"I sent you as a cherub to protect and guard over the holy mountain I have created. You wandered amongst sparkling gemstones."

(Book of Ezekiel 28:14)

"Your beauty made you proud, your riches veiled your wisdom. Now — learn from it."

(*Book of Ezekiel 28:17*)

Prayer for Samech from Psalm 119:113-120:

113 "I see through double-minded men,
I AM the love of Your Light.
114 You are my refuge and my shield;
I AM the might of Your word.
115 May all earthly shadows
become stars in Your sky.
116 I live in Your Light and blessings,
I AM the fulfillment of all needs;
my gratitude dances to Your song of grace.
117 I merge with Your pillar of salvation;
Your love is my life.
118 Those who have hardened their hearts
cannot feel Your Light.
119 But Your Presence transforms all illusions;
my hands and heart receive Your guidance.
120 My body trembles, merging with You;
I stand in awe of Your eternal love."

16

7

AYIN

ע

SIGHT & INSIGHT
The Fall of the Temple

The Wounded Healer. Inner Change. Libertion through Transformation. Destroyer and Renewer. Redemption through Repentance. To rebuild the Temple in three days.

Tiphareth – Hod	Grace – Presence
Gematria	70
Tarot	The Tower

PERSONALITY

The number of the broken heart. A gifted healer through experience. 16 is therefore usually a gifted healer who understands the problems of a broken heart. 16 stands for spiritual trust, hope and love. 16 has to face many tests and trials, but, through them, finds the resources to raise him/herself up by faith and to help others.

SEED
16

You were standing at the edge, staring into the abyss, when the master asked you to step forward to give yourself UP in order for you to experience trust while facing the void. You hesitated for a moment, then you gave in and let yourself go, freefalling through the spheres of loss and human suffering. Then suddenly, you felt wings unfold on your back, floating safely into the hands of the master. You GAVE UP your pain, pride and hopelessness, and were given joy, forgiveness and trust instead. Now this is the healing you have come to share with anyone who needs it.

"I praise the Lord with all my heart! I rejoice in God, my Savior, because He has chosen me, his humble servant. All future generations will call me blessed. He punishes all those with pride in their hearts and scatters them to the wind. He topples the princes of the world from their thrones, but exalts the humble. He feeds the hungry with good things, but the rich he sends empty-handed away."

(*Gospel of Luke 1:46-48 & 51-52*)

A Prayer for Ayin from Psalm 119:121-128:

121 "I live my life in Your Light;
I AM the union of all opposites.
122 Your blessings fill my days and nights;
any shadow transforms in Your grace.
123 I AM the enfolding of Your salvation,
here and now and forevermore.
124 Your guidance of love and wisdom
directs my words and ways.
125 I merge with my gifts and purpose;
Your Light is with me always.
126 I call for Your Presence
whenever Your vibration is forgotten.
127 The rays of my love
radiate like the sun of suns,
128 and Your embrace of wisdom
opens the gate to the Way of the Heart."

17

6

PEH

פ

SPEECH & SILENCE
The Savior

(P, F) (Prime) Awakening. Guidance. Hope.
Healing. Purity in Illumination.

Netzah – Hod	Victory – Presence
Gematria	80
Tarot	The Star

PERSONALITY

The lucky number 17 stands for goodness achieved through countless tests and difficulties, both
in this life and earlier lives. 17s are blessed after
having passed and understood these tests. Having
achieved wisdom through their own experience,

they can now enjoy the gifts of life and funda-
mental goodness. 17 is the peace after a storm,
and the forgiveness after an argument.

SEED
17

You stood next to Yeshua in the river Jordan
when he was being baptized and became the
Savior. There he was initiated to take upon
him the burdens of his fellow men. Through
the trials and tribulations that followed, he
was purified and made ready for the final test,
the transformation of man. Now you have
come to share with your fellow men how they
must prepare and purify themselves through
the trials and tribulations of life, so that
they, too, can be reborn and ego-free, even
in this incarnation.

"Say Yes, when you mean Yes – and No, when
you mean No! All else is confusion."
(*Gospel of Matthew* 5:37)

"And in that place I saw the fountains of righteousness, which were inexhaustible; and around it were many fountains of wisdom; and all thirsty drank of them, and were filled with wisdom, and their dwellings were with the righteous and holy and elect. And at that hour the Son of Man was named in the presence of the Lord of Spirits, and his name before the Head of Days. Yea, before the sun and the signs were created, before the stars of the heavens were made, his name was named before the Lord of Spirits. He shall be a staff to the righteous whereon to stay themselves and not fall, and he shall be the Light of the Gentiles, and the hope of those who are troubled of heart. All who dwell on Earth shall fall down and worship before him, and will praise and bless and celebrate with song the Lord of Spirits. And for this reason hath he been chosen, before the creation of the world and for evermore."

(Enoch 48:1-6)

"The father of Truth is the sun and its mother is the moon; the wind (Holy Spirit) carried it in its womb; whilst the Earth nourished it."

(The Emerald Tablet 4)

"This is the guild of the Heavenly Warrior. Heaven and Earth are my parents, consciousness my home. Absence of selfishness is my sword, simplicity my way. Patience and joy are my strength, presence and authenticity my hallmark. Gracefully I dance through life providing help where it is needed."

(The Prophecy of Freya)

"Everything created by God longs to share in the glory destined for His children. All creation lives under the yoke of transience, not because creation wishes it, but because of its inertia. There is, however, hope. All created things will one day be set free from this hopeless enslavement and take their place in the glory and freedom that belongs to God's children."

(Letter to the Romans 8:19-22)

Prayer for Peh from Psalm 119:129-136:

129 "Your Presence is filled with blessings;
I open my heart like a flower.
130 I AM the unfolding of Your word;
may all questions be placed into its light.
131 I speak and breathe
within Your love and guidance.
132 Your fields of grace are my home;
Your name is the open seal of my heart.
133 Direct my steps in the Light of Your word;
I AM the transformation of all error or illusion.
134 I AM the peace and freedom I seek;
Your love abides in my very being.
135 Your face shines upon my body and soul,
Your eternal Light is my guide.
136 All sadness vanishes in Your Presence;
I AM the victory of Your Light."

18

TZADIK

JUSTICE & HUMILITY
The Virgin Mother

(Ts, Tz) Humility. Intuition. Through the Gates. Prayer. Nourishment.

Netzah – Yesod	Victory – Foundation
Gematria	90
Tarot	The Moon

PERSONALITY

18 represents the tension between the spiritual and the material. 18s will often find themselves in the centre of battlegrounds, as a target for the anger of contending parties. As such, they have to learn to counter evil with goodness, and to show magnanimity and forgiveness.

In the dark and moonless night, the Mother of all Innocence and Purity was smeared and ridiculed. You were there, witnessing this degrading act of arrogance, stupidity and darkness. The Mother kept silent. But it was not the Mother who was degraded or ridiculed, it was the arrogant, the stupid and the darkness behind the smearing. Later in the night, the full moon broke through the dark clouds, exposing it all for everyone to see, showing how justice always follows humility and forgiveness. Now you have come into this world to bear witness to the Mother of All Innocence and Her values of Truth, Love and Compassion.

"When I talk to a prophet, I usually do so through visions and dreams, but that is not the way I communicate with my servant Moses. He is the faithful leader of my people. I talk to him face to face and not in riddles. He has seen me as I am. Therefore, how dare you contradict him?"

(Book of Numbers 12:6-9)

Prayer for Tzadik from Psalm 119:137-144:

137 "I rejoice in Your Presence,
Your truth and Your Light.
138 The emissions of Your love
are my guides.
139 If I have been outside of mySelf,
I AM the remembrance of Your Light.
140 My heart knows Your ways of wisdom;
their precious pearls are my eternal joy.
141 When clouds of trouble darken my day,
I call on Your love and guidance.
142 Your everlasting Light
is my only truth.
143 In both joy and distress
I delight in Your words and ways.
144 Your seeds are forever sacred.
I AM the union of the One."

19

4

QOPH

ק

HOLINESS & CYCLE
The Christ Child

(Q) (Prime) Prince/Princess of Heaven.
Innocence. Vitality. Energy. New Life.

Netzah – Malkoota	Victory – Queendom
Gematria	100
Tarot	The Sun

PERSONALITY

The masculine in woman and the feminine in man,
19 symbolizes the opposite you aspire to and
long to be united with. 19 radiates health and
vitality, and integrates all opposites, becoming one
and whole.

When the Christ Child is being born, when a heightened and evolved consciousness is being manifested in the world, everything stands still in awe and gratitude – caught for a moment in eternity outside time and space. It is like a held-back breath, or a sparrow held in mid-air. You were one of the shepherds visiting the crib to adorate the newborn master. You saw the White Dove descending from above, hovering over the child, blessing it. You are that blessing, and you have come here to share its essence with the world and every living being in it, so they, too, may understand, that they all carry the Christ Child within, and that It is being brought forth by gratitude for All that is.

"May that which is below be as the reality above, and may that which is above be as the reality below, so that everything may attain the miracle of Unity."
(*The Emerald Tablet 2*)

"I come from the first, self-made Light of Unity to tell about it and disseminate it to everyone."

(*The Wisdom of Jesus Christ*)

"Judge them by their actions, just as one judges a tree by its fruits. Grapes do not grow on a thorn bush, neither are figs to be found on a thistle."

(*Gospel of Matthew 7:16*)

Prayer for Qoph from Psalm 119:145-152:

145 "I sing with all my heart and soul; welcome!
I AM Your love fulfilled.
146 I rejoice in Your Presence
and thrive in the nearness of Your Light.
147 I raise all darkness with Your helping hand;
I stand on the holy mountain of Your word.
148 I AM the open door that never closes,
I merge with Your Light by day and night.
149 My voice speaks the vibration of Your love;
my life is carried in the arms of Your wisdom.
150 If wickedness arrives, I send it away;
but never too far from Your love and blessings.
151 You are with me always and forever,
I AM the truth of Your Light.
152 My whole being knows Your Presence
and walks with Its Light through eternity."

20

3

RESH

RISE & FALL
Resurrection

(R) Awakening. Renewal. Forgiveness. Truth and Consequence. The Phoenix Rising.

Hod – Yesod	Presence – Foundation
Gematria	200
Tarot	Judgment

PERSONALITY

The number 20 represents awakening. Just like 2, it is an expression of duality and psychic abilities, as well as daydreams. Dreams are to be realized in the now. 20s can find it hard to achieve material success.

On the third day, you were one in the group of mourners, who came to minister to the body of the master, but found his tomb empty. You were told by an angel, sitting outside the grave, that the master wasn't there anymore but that he had risen. In that moment you were shown how the master had descended to the lowest spheres in order to free the lost souls there and how he, through the power of forgiveness, had purified and freed them all. In that way you were shown how genuine Love and Compassion are the keys to renewal, resurrection and everlasting life. Now you have come to share this knowledge with your fellow men.

"I am Resurrection
A healer who leaves no trace
I pray and walk in silence
Invisible by Your grace."

(*The God Formula*)

"In the same way as the Father raises people from the dead and gives them new life, the Son also gives new life to whomsoever he will. The Father judges no-one, but hands over every pronouncement of sentence to the Son."

(Gospel of John 5:21-22)

"The dead shall live, their bodies shall arise. Those who dwell in the dust shall awake and sing, for Thy dew is a dew of Light."

(Book of Isaiah 26:19)

"And in his spiritual form he visited the spirits of the dead, which were held captive and he preached the message to them."

(1st Epistle of Peter 3:19)

"But those who accepted him and believed in him were given the right to call themselves the children of God. They were born again. This is not a physical or human birth, but a divine birth."

(Gospel of John 1:12-13)

Prayer for Resh from Psalm 119:153-160:

153 "Fill all suffering with Your love;
I AM the remembrance of Your Light.
154 Bless my days and raise my way;
hold my life in the grace of Your hands.
155 I AM the power of Your word
that reaches the divided and the united.
156 I AM the might of Your compassion;
my life enfolds in the course of Your love.
157 If foes or friends join my path,
I abide in the glory of Your Presence.
158 I meet the faithless with compassion,
for they do not remember Your Light.
159 I AM the communion with Your wisdom;
direct my life within Your love.
160 Truth and grace dwell in Your words.
Your Presence shines forth Its eternal Light."

21

SHIN

DIVINE GRACE & SCRIPTURE
Holy Spirit

(Sh) Catharsis. Faith. Trust. Responsibility.

Hod – Malkoota	Presence – Queendom
Gematria	300
Tarot	The World

PERSONALITY

Due to the integration of 1's will and origina-
lity with 2's dreams and visions, 21 is assured of
victory, wealth and prosperity. The only thing that
can stand in the way of 21's success is his/her
ignorance of the true workings behind it. Everything given to a 21 must be shared. To understand
this is what makes 21's world go round.

SEED
21

You were among the disciples when the master proclaimed that "you can ridicule me and the Heavenly Source of All Being, but you may never ever ridicule the Holy Spirit." In that moment you understood that the Holy Spirit is the Comforter sent to guide humanity from now on, into the future. You were shown Its divine grace and sacred power, which is holding and connecting everything created together as One. This is the power behind any creational process and without it there would be no physical or etheric existence. It is by that divine grace that Truth, Love and Compassion are being distributed everywhere, activating and nourishing the Sacred Seed within all living beings. Now you have come to tell and teach your fellow men about it.

"Let us, therefore, step unhesitatingly before God's throne, because He will, in His grace and mercy, come to our aid in our time of need."

(Epistle to the Hebrews 4:16)

"Be not carried away by false doctrines. It is good for our hearts to be strengthened by the power of grace." *(Epistle to the Hebrews 13:9)*

"Three times I asked the Lord to remove it, but He said to me: 'My grace is all you have, for my power attains its purpose through helplessness." *(2nd Epistle to the Corinthians 12:8)*

Prayer for Shin from Psalm 119:161-168:

161 "If I should either be lifted or bruised,
my heart will always sing Your song.
162 I rejoice in Your Presence
which enfolds immeasurable gifts.
163 I let go of all falsehood
as I love Your Light.
164 Seven times a day I unite
Your guidance with my being.
165 I AM the mighty fountain of peace
that fills all who unseal Your wisdom.
166 I receive Your salvation
and follow Your way.
167 I radiate Your Light,
for I AM love.
168 I keep Your Light in my heart and home
and walk all my ways in Your Presence."

22

TAV

ת

TRUTH & PERFECTION
The True Servant, The Master Builder

Master number. (Th) Removing the Veil Between the Worlds. Manifesting from Ether to Earth. Grace. Generosity.

Yesod – Malkoota	Foundation – Queendom
Gematria	400
Tarot	The Truth

PERSONALITY

22 possesses 4's stability while at the same time representing a doubling up of 2's feeling for dreams and visions. There are 22 letters in the Aramaic and Hebrew alphabets. 22 can have lots

of ideas, but needs to find a way to express them clearly and distinctly in order for others to be able to understand them. It is up to 22 to create his or her own future and success. Problems only arise if 22 becomes lazy.

22 is the most powerful of all the numbers. It is often called the "Master Builder". 22 has the ability to transform the most ambitious dream into reality. It is potentially the most successful of all numbers. It has many of 11's intuitive and inspired insights, combined with 4's practical and methodical nature.

22 has no boundaries, yet is nevertheless disciplined. 22 sees all archetypes and brings them down to Earth, where their essence can be manifested in some form or another. 22's opportunities are wasted if the bearer of this number avoids working practically with them. Just like 11, 22 can easily shrink away from opportunities and thus create inner pressure for themselves. Both 11 and 22 tend to experience both great responsibility and great stress, especially when young. 22 always needs to work toward realizing goals that are larger and wider-reaching than personal ambition. 22 serves the world by manifesting spirituality and spiritual science, but in a practical way. 22 is an outstanding creator. 22 is always working toward 33.

SEED
22

You stood on top of Mount Carmel when everything was created, full of gratitude, looking over the land, seeing the beauty and perfection of it all. You saw how everything was interconnected to fit into a whole, and that each and every part would be nothing without it. You lit a fire on the mountaintop, the Light of Truth, which must shine forever and by which new beings and universes will be created and sanctified. You are the one who came to keep the fire burning and to share its deepest wisdom of Truth, Love and Compassion with the world.

"When He placed His image in all created things, I was with Him and He was pleased with me every day and I exulted with Him, rejoiced to see the wide earth, to see mankind being created."

(Book of Proverbs 8:27 & 30-31)

"If I speak in tongues of men or of angels but do not have love, I am only a resounding gong or a clanging cymbal. If I have the gift of prophecy and can fathom all mysteries and all knowledge, and I have a faith that can move mountains, but do not have love, I am nothing. If I give all I possess to the poor and give my body to hardship that I may boast, but do not have love, I gain nothing. Love is patient, love is kind. It does not envy, it does not boast, it is not proud. It does not dishonor others, it is not self-seeking, it is not easily angered, it keeps no record of wrongs. Love does not delight in evil but rejoices with the truth. It always protects, always trusts, always hopes, always perseveres."

(Corinthians 13)

"I am Alpha and Omega, the first and the last, the beginning and the end of all things."

(Book of Revelation 22:13)

Prayer for Tav from Psalm 119:169-176:

169 "I AM the answer to every call,
and the understanding of all questions.
170 I AM the advent of Your grace;
Your love stills every storm in my heart.
171 My lips overflow with praise,
for Your wisdom fills my very being.
172 My tongue and heart sing Your word,
for You are the Light, the truth and the way.
173 Your hand is my help and my home;
Your Presence completes every choice I make.
174 I AM the realization of Your blessings;
Your love is my delight.
175 I AM the praise of Your glory,
Your Light overflows throughout my life.
176 I AM the return to Your Presence,
now and for evermore."

33

DAAT
Christ

לג

Master number. The Open Heart.
The Number of Horus. Truth and Transformation.

PERSONALITY

Even more fortunate than 24, 33 reflects a doubling up of positive, constructive, optimistic, creative and loving energy. It is the most influential of all the numbers. It is the Master Teacher. 33 combines 11 and 22 and raises their potential to a new level of freedom in generosity and gratitude. When 33 expresses his or her potential fully, they are freed from any kind of personal ambition and can focus their vast potential on the spiritual awakening of humankind.

The number 33 inspires extraordinary confidence due to the great level of dedication and devotion that characterizes this person. This is apparent in their tireless search to acquire insight and wisdom before teaching others. A 33 person at full strength is rarely to be found. If 33 isn't brought to maturity, or doesn't consciously seek to become mature, they will be reduced to a 6. A 33, brought to full maturity, however, embodies the archetype of the bodhisattva, the servant of mankind.

SEED
33

The golden substance, which can be seen and felt in the ether, is the "second coming" of Christ. Christ is, above all, a consciousness of the highest order, which is spreading like wildfire in the ether, where it awaits the awakening of human hearts. It is through the heart that man shall experience and unfold the Law of Light, which is Truth, Love and Compassion on Earth. You were sent here to spread the good news among people, and, in that way, prepare their hearts for the "second coming", which is already here, waiting for man to start to practice its precepts.

"Whenever goodness ceases to exist and injustice seizes power, I incarnate myself as an Avatar on Earth. Age after age, I reveal myself in order to protect the righteous, destroy the wicked and establish the truth."

(Bhagavad Gita, 4:7-8)

THE NUMBERS FROM
23 to 100

NOTE: To some of the numbers I have attached words in Aramaic with the same gematria value as the number in question. In the tradition of the Essenes, all words or concepts that share the same value are somehow connected. Use your intuition in order to experience how these words apply to you.

23
FULL ACTION IN EVERY CAPACITY
(Prime). *Chayyah*: Life. *Chiah*: That part of the Soul that is linked to Hochmah (Wisdom). *Zuta*: Less.

23 is the number that releases spiritual gifts, as long as there is belief and trust. 21 also represents physical wellbeing, health, wealth and happiness. King David's Psalm 23 in the Old Testament expresses gratitude for being able to thank the

Heavenly Source of All Being, regardless of the problems one might have. 23 is the number of humility, the realization that the most important thing in life is to do good and serve humankind with unconditional love.

24 RIPENING

Dakh: Oppressed. *Kadh*: Receptacle. Fortune's number. A gift for good karma.

24 will bring happiness and good fortune to all relationships. Like 6, it is a number whose magnetic goodness comes from the ability to give and receive love. 24 has to be careful not to become arrogant and selfish. If 24 practices generosity, his/her life will become a river, flowing with wealth on all levels.

25 SATISFACTION

Chioa: The Animal.

Open to the highest aspects of existence, 25 has to do with learning and analysis. The success of a 25 is dependent on his/her ability to learn through their own experiences. 25 contains the number 7. Like the 7, it must be aware and take care of all things financial.

26 MULTIPLYING

YHVH: Yehova. *Kabedh*: To honour.

26 is especially blessed by faith, service and trust in the Heavenly Source of All Being. The numerical value of the four Hebrew letters composing the name YHVH in the Bible is 26.

A person carrying 26 within themselves must develop the highest, most honest of characters. 26 expects perfection, isn't deceitful and doesn't tell lies. One can always trust in a 26.

26 contains the number 8, which indicates that 26 has entered his/her incarnation with a mission of obtaining integrity. That mission is to eradicate every lie and deception. If it succeeds, 26 will always be magically protected and endowed with good fortune.

27 SELF-KNOWLEDGE

Zak: Pure, clear, transparent, innocent.

"When you become as children once again, you will enter the Kingdom". Purity and simplicity in thought. Eternal youth. Naivety, innocence and peace. This state will be sustained as long as 27 reposes in him/herself and does no harm.

28 BLESSING

(Perfect). *Chekh*: Palate. *Koch*: Power. *Tit*: Clay. *Yadid*: A loved one. *Yichudh*: Union with God.

28 represents strength and dedication. It has the same energy as 10 and 19, but with extra power and energy to fight for true honesty and integrity. 28 has the ability to transform hate and bitterness into love, forgiveness, peace and understanding.

When 28 has learned, through his/her own experience, how painful dishonesty and mistrust can be, and therefore learns the value of forgiveness, they will be endowed with great success and fortune.

29 HOLDING

(Prime). A number that has a tendency to attract heavy and mournful energies, 29 is rather quick to take on other people's mistakes and problems.

29 is very easily influenced, so it is important he/she avoids outer influences like TV or other artificial stimulants that affect the senses. 29 needs to stop daydreaming.

30 COMMUNICATING – GIVING

This is the number for both peaceful and intellectual thoughts. 30 possesses the ability to come to the right conclusions by analyzing all the facts. 30 is a purely cognitive and intellectual number, which works best alone, doesn't need many friends and is of a meditative nature.

31 SELF-BUILDING

(Prime). *El*: Holy name.
An intellectual genius who tends to live in seclusion. 31 has to learn to share with others.

32 EFFECTING

Ehyahweh: A combination between the macro and micro cosmos. *Kadobh*: Center.

32 is the number of love, wholeness, the healing of two broken halves, and two equal partners who are in harmony.

34 UNFOLDING

The number of the priest/priestess. An opener to the spiritual realms. Like 7, 34 is an intuitive creative who will make a good counselor. *See 7 & 25.*

35 ACCOMPLISHMENT

Agla: A name for God. *Ateh Gibor le-Olam Adonai*: Oh Lord, You are the Almighty in Eternity. *Elad*: Shem ha-Mephorash's 10th name. *See 26.*

36 PEACE

Badhal: To share, to divide. *Eloha*: The Heavenly Source of All Being.

Despite 3's optimism and energy, together with 6's wealth and love, a 36 must stay centered.

37 ARTISTIC CAPABILITY

(Prime) *Akaiah* (day angel). *Degel*: Banner. *Hebel*: Abel, son of Adam. Vanity.

37 is in the same family as 10, but while 28 is on the positive side of 10, 37 represents the negative side. A 37 therefore has to be aware of the need to focus on positive thoughts, not negative feelings.

38 SOLVING

Chel: Bulwark, bastion. *Chol*: Desecrate. *Lach*: Damp, fresh, green. *See 11 & 29.*

39 HARVEST

Tal: Dew. *YHVH Achad*: YHVH is One.

39 is a number of opposites. It is in the same family as 3 and carries the challenges of 12.

40 PROVING – TESTING

Chalav: Milk.

In the same family as 31 and 4 on a higher plane.

41 ENJOYING

(Prime) *Em*: Mother. *Zebhul*: Dwelling in the fourth heaven. *See 32.*

42 PLEASURE – AWARENESS

Ama: Mother. *Ayel*: Angel of the first astrological house. *Bilhah*: Rachel's handmaiden, mother of Dan. *Levo*: Shem ha-Mephorash's 19th name. *Vaval*: Shem ha Mephorash's 43rd name.

42 is a holy number that has good karma. It should bring good possibilities and happiness. However, 42s must be careful not to be too arrogant and self-righteous, otherwise their stream of gifts and energy may become blocked.

43 STEWARDSHIP

(Prime) *Gadhol*: Great, large. *Gam*: Together. *Lehach*: Shem ha-Mephorash's 34th name. *Yedidiah*: One who is beloved of God, Solomon.

43 has the same energy as 16, 25 and 34.

44 ANSWERED – DONE

Dam: Blood. *Deli*: Receptacle, Aquarius. *Giel*: Angel of the third astrological house. *Taleh*: Lamb, the Ram. Intuition. 44 is in the same family as 26.

45 BELIEF

Adam: Man. *Adhom*: Red. *Lot*: Lot. *Yelah*: Shem ha-Mephorash's 44th name.

The number of purity and simplicity, full of peace, innocence and eternal youth. 45 represents forgiving and living a harmless life.

46 ACCOMPLISHING EVERYWHERE

Bedhil: Tin. *Dameb*: Shem ha-Mephorash's 65th name. *Hahahel* (day angel). *Meah*: Hundreds. *Toel*: Angel of the second astrological house. *Yahel*: Angel of the seventh astrological house. *See 37.*

47 SETTLEMENT

(Prime) *Aum*: Shem ha-Mephorash's 30th name. *Veyel*: Angel of the sixth astrological house. *Mebah*: Shem ha-Mephorash's 14th name. *Mabeh*: Shem ha-Mephorash's 55th name. *Yezel*: Shem ha-Mephorash's 13th name. *See 29.*

48 PERFECT – POTENTIAL

Cham: Ham, Noah's son. *Kokab*: Star, Mercury. *Vameb*: Shem ha-Mephorash's 61st name. *Vehuel* (day angel). *See 30.*

49 FULFILLMENT OF BLESSING

Hagiel: Intelligence of Venus. *See 31.*

50 RETURN

Adamah: Earth. *Aldiath* (night angel). *Dagh Gadhol*: Large fish. *Yam*: Ocean. *Yeli*: Shem ha-Mephorash's 2nd name. *Yeyal*: Shem ha-Mephorash's 58th name. 50 is like 5 on a higher plane.

51 DANCING

Edom: Edom. *Nogah*: Light. *See 6.*

52 DEVOTION

Anima: The great Mother. *Ben*: Son. *Lekab*: Shem ha-Mephorash's 31st name. *Magog*: Magog. *Yebem*: Shem ha-Mephorash's 70th name.

The prophet Elijah's number for perfection, which only begins to function when it is transcended or works in a different reality than the physical. 52 is even more sensitive, open and innocent then 16, the number of the Broken Heart. 52 can be seduced and lose sense of reality. 52 is the number of selfless dedication and devotion.

53 BEYOND

(Prime) *Eben*: Stone. *Gan*: Garden. *Haziel* (day angel). *See 8*.

54 CYCLES – INTERACTION

Dan: Israeli tribe. *Mattah*: Tribe, branch, root, staff, sceptre. *Nedh*: Pile, wall. *See 9*.

55 WHOLENESS – RESPONSIBILITY

Kaltha: Bride, feminine principle. *Miah*: Shem ha-Mephorash's 48th name. *Noah*: Magnificent, eminent. *See 10*.

56 RESPONSE

Akhlah: Give birth. *Nun*: Egyptian goddess. *Yom*: Day. *See 11*.

57 GIVING

On: Strength, wealth, sorrow. *Banah*: To build. *Dagim*: Fish. *Motev*: Better. *Luviah*: Scorpio (day angel). *Vavaliah*: Taurus (day angel).

A lucky number that heralds good times and bread on the table.

58 FAITH

Chen: Grace, elegance, charm. *Lehchiah* (night angel). *Mechi*: Battering ram, Shem ha-Mephorash's 64th name. *Noach*: Noah. *Taliahad*: Angel of water. *Yeaazel* (night angel).

This number attracts help when needed.

59 ABILITY – FRUIT

(Prime). *See 14*.

60 FREEDOM

Halakhal: Praxis regarding the Talmud. *Ni*: Complaint. *Keli*: Shem ha-Mephorash's 18th name.

The same as 6, but closer to the original starting point 0 = the Void. No attachments, no limitations, no need for approval or applause.

61 PERFECTION – COMPLETION

(Prime) *Ani*: Shem ha-Mephorash's 37th name. *Damabiah* (day angel).

The number of the communicator, a 61 works best in synergy with others. They have a charismatic power that can influence many but they must beware of addiction, not least to one's own charisma.

62 REALITY

Asa: A king of Judah. *Ben*: Between.

The number of maturity and experience. A 62 insists on keeping a level head and avoids unnecessary worry. They must stay away from all forms of projection, accept responsibility and solve problems. Challenges for a 62 might be stagnation, resistance, postponement and/or reticence.

63 INTERACTION

Boneh: Builder. *Navi*: Prophet.

63 represents balance, reformation, mission, sovereignty and a regenerating quality. A 63 can be compassioned and achieve liberation but be too idealistic.

64 RESPONSIBILITY

Dani: Shem ha-Mephorash's 50th name. *Din*: Justice. *Gonah*: Serenity. *Nogah*: Venus.

64 can often mean success at first, but disappointment later. It can also mean a strong personality, consequence, manifestation, hard work, charisma and truth. A 64 should be aware of their ego and avoid feeding it.

65 THE CHOSEN

Adonai: My Lord. *Hekel*: Temple. *Dumiah*: Silence. *Leleah*: Shem ha-Mephorash's 6th name.

A solid base that allows one to take chances, while retaining a guarantee of protection. 65 is Adonai's number, the Holy Guardian Angel. It represents charisma, calm, breakthrough, elevation and transformation.

66 HARMONY

Clio: Greek muse. *Yaven*: Moor.

The double 6 means that a 66 is created to foster harmony around them.

67 NEW BEGINNING

(Prime) *Abidan*: Prince of the tribe of Benyamin. *Binah*: Awareness. *Elul*: The 12th month of the Jewish calendar. *Zayin*: Sword, 6th letter of the alphabet.

67 represents spiritual awakening and new beginnings, and is connected to 13 and transfiguration.

68 BALANCE

Chayim: Life.

68 represents stability through change and movement – and freedom. A 68 is gifted with visionary abilities, but needs to find the balance between pure vision and illusion.

69 MERGING

The Bridal Chamber. The merging of the feminine and the masculine.

70 PERFECTION

Adam ve-Ghavvah: Adam and Eve. *Gog ve-Magog*: Gog and Magog. *Ken*: Honesty. *Mik*: Shem ha-Mephorash's 42nd name.

70 is connected to wholeness; 7 on a higher plane.

71 ENDURANCE

(Prime) *Elil*: Idol, image. *Mille*: To fill. *Yonah*: Dove, Jonah. $7 + 1 = 8$.

71 needs to find his/her path but must remember that not all paths are equally inspiring.

72 GOODNESS

Gilgul: Reincarnation, transmigration.

The number of goodness, Chesed in the Kabbalah. 72 is accompanied by a heavenly blessing. In the kabbalistic *Zohar*, there are 72 names for God.

73 PERFECTION – TRUTH

(Prime) *Gimel*: Camel. *Hochmah*: Wisdom. *See 10.*

74 CREATIVITY

Adh: Eternity, perseverance. *Edh*: Witness, evidence,

yardstick. *Dea*: Knowledge, wisdom. *Gihon*: River in the Garden of Eden. *Lemed*: Ox.

74 is good at making the intangible tangible. Adding 7 and 4 gives 11, which offers greater creative and artistic opportunities.

75 HUMILITY

Helel: Clarity, morning star, Lucifer. *Kohen*: Priest. *Laylah*: Night. *Melah*: Shem ha-Mephorash's 23rd name. *Mikah*: Micah. *See 12*.

76 CHANGE

Abedh: Servant. *Elilah*: Goddess. *See 13*.

77 PROTECTION

Ez: Goat. *Oz*: Strength, power, violence, glory. *Mazel*: Destiny, good fortune.

A lucky number. When 77 is strong and patient, goodness, honesty and perseverance triumph over arrogance, deception and falsity. A 77 always needs to be aware of the relationships he/she enters into and resist a tendency to take shortcuts.

78 HONESTY

Aiwass: The name of the Law Giver. *Chalam*: To dream. *Chelem*: A dream. *Hekel Ahbah*: The Palace of Love, Heaven's dwelling. *Melach*: Salt. *Yezalel* (day angel). *Zamael*: Angel for Mars. *See 15.*

79 LIBERATION

(Prime) *Adah*: Lamech's wife. *Boaz*: Column in Solomon's temple. *Yachin*: Column in Solomon's temple. *Delilah*: Samson's nemesis. *Golem*: Shapeless mass, artificial person. *Sit*: Shem ha-Mephorash's 3rd name. *Vemibael* (day angel). *See 16.*

80 ETERNITY

Yesod: The Cornerstone. *Hehau*: Shem ha-Mephorash's 12th name. *Kalal*: to make perfect. *Kes*: Throne. 8 on a higher plane.

81 ATONEMENT

Anoki: I. *Aph*: Anger, nose. *Aya*: Shem ha-Mephorash's 67th name; that which is forever. *Yelayel* (night angel). *See 9.*

82 STRENGTH

Anael: Venusian Angel. *Lavan*: White.

82 is a powerful number, denoting strength, courage, transformation and change. It can even transform hate into love.

83 CLAIRVOYANCE

(Prime) *Ebelim*: Regrets. *Pag*: Unripe fig. *See 11*.

84 WHOLENESS

Achlamah: Amethyst. *Chalom*: A dream. *Chanokh*: Enoch.

The number of wholeness. Jewish astrology divides the span of a lifetime into 12 sections of 7 years each, which gives 84 years in total.

85 GENEROSITY

Peh: Mouth. *Milah*: Circumcision. *See 4*.

86 JUSTICE

Haleluyah: Hallelujah, praised be the Almighty. *Mavedil*: To divide. *Mum*: Shem ha-Mephorash's 72nd name.

God's holy number. The ultimate number of karma that guarantees precise recompense. As you sow, so shall you reap.

87 REDEMPTION

Levanah: The moon. *Bihelami* (day angel). *Paz*: Pure gold. *See 15*.

88 UNCONDITIONAL TRUST

Chaph: Pure, innocent. *Pach*: Trap, danger.

Like 16 except that 88 prompts humility.

89 SILENCE

(Prime) *Demamah*: Calm, whisper. *Taph*: Children. *See 17*.

90 FAITH

Lamekh: Lamech. *Mem*: Water. *Domem*: Quiet.

The correct angle. Number of the phallus. 9 on a higher plane.

91 HOPE

Kelali: Universal, collective. *Man*: Manna. *Malakh*: Angel. *Malka*: Queen. *Sael*: Shem ha-Mephorash's 45th name.

Blessed hope. When all seems hopeless, 91 always comes to the rescue. See *Psalm 91 (Old Testament)*.

92 WISDOM

Aniel: Aquarius (day angel). *Botz*: Mud. *Pachad*: Fear. *See 11.*

93 SINCERITY

Magen: Defence, shield. *Megen*: Defender. *Tzava*: Host, army. *See 3.*

94 INSIDE-OUT

Madim: Mars. *Mazzel Tov*: Congratulations, good luck. *Menadh*: Shem ha-Mephorash's 36th name. *See 13.*

95 CHARITY

Daniel: Ram (night angel). *Malkah*: Queen. *Zebulun*: Israeli tribe. *See 14.*

96 TRANSCENDING LIMITATIONS

Lehahel (angel). *Tzav*: Rule. *See 15.*

97 HEALER

(Prime) *Haniel*: Archangel. *Tzahov*: Yellow. *See 16.*

98 LUCK

Chetz: Arrow. *Tzach*: Clear. *See 17.*

99 REDEMPTION

See 9 & 18.

100 SANCTITY

Kaph: Palm. *Loa*: Throat. *Mas*: A disease. *Nelakh*: Shem ha-Mephorash's 21st name. *Pakh*: Bottle. *Sam*: Spice, medication, poison. *Tzi*: Dryness, ship. *See 1 & 10.*

200 HIGHER CONSCIOUSNESS

Etzem: Bone, substance, essence, body. *Qayitz*: Summer. *Qesem*: The power of prophecy. *See 20.*

300 SPIRIT

Ruach Elohim: God's Spirit (Holy Spirit). *Qar*: Cold, quiet. *Raq*: Thin. *Roq*: Spit. *See 21.*

345 MYSTIC

El Shaddai: God the Almighty. *Mahash*: Shem ha-Mephorash's 5th name. *Mosheh*: Moses. *See 3 & 12.*

365 REPETITION

Neshiah: Oblivion.
Enoch's life span. *See 14.*

400 PRAYER

Ashel: Shem ha-Mephorash's 47th name. *Kashaph*: Sorceress. *Nashim*: Women, wives. *Qash*: Straw. *Saq*: Sack. *Sekhelim*: Intelligence. *Shanim*: Year. *Shenaim*: Two. *See 22.*

Heavenly Source of All Being,
May the embrace of Your Light guide me,
now and forevermore.
I walk in the way.
May the might of Your endless love
fill all space and time.
I AM the Light of the world.
May the lines of Light open,
connecting all beings as Brothers and Sisters.
WE ARE the union of Light.
May grace fill our voices, hearts and hands.
Always.

NALEEA

BIBLIOGRAPHY

Auken, John Van & Miller, Ruben, *Edgar Cayce on the Mysterious Essenes*, A.R.E. Press 2016

Blech, Benjamin, *The Secret of Hebrew Words*, Jason Aronson 2001

Crossway, *Study Bible, English Standard Version*, Crossway 2001

DeConick, April D., *The Original Gospel of Thomas in Translation*, T & T Clark 2006

Diringer, David, *The Alphabet*, Hutchinson's Publications 1930

Ginsburgh, Rabbi Yitzchak, *The Alef-Beit*, Jason Aronson Inc. 1991

Godwin, David, *Cabalistic Encyclopedia*, Llewellyn Publications 2004

Khan, Hazret Inayat, *The Complete Sayings*, Sufi Order Publishing, 1978

Kushner, Lawrence, *The Book of Letters*, Jewish Light Publishing 1990

Layton, Bentley, *The Gnostic Scriptures,* Doubleday & Co 1987

Muhl, Lars, *The God Formula,* Gilalai Publishing 2020

Muhl, Lars, *The Law of Light,* Watkins Publishing 2014

Muhl, Lars, *The Light Within a Human Heart,* Watkins Publishing 2022

Muhl, Lars, *The Wisdom of a Broken Heart,* Watkins Publishing 2021

d'Olivet, Fabre, *The Hebraic Tongue Restored,* Samuel Weiser 1921

Place, Robert M., *The Alchemical Tarot 6th Edition,* Hermes Publications 2021

Sanderfur, Glenn, *Lives of The Master,* A.R.E. Press 1988

Schonfield, Hugh, *The Essene Odyssey,* Element Books 1984

Taylor, Joan E., *The Essenes, the Scrolls and the Dead Sea,* Oxford University Press 2012

Vermes, Geza, *The Complete Dead Sea Scrolls in English,* Penguin Press 1962

Wedder, M. & Thompson, J., *Ivan Pannin's Numerics in Scripture,* New England Bible Sales 2014

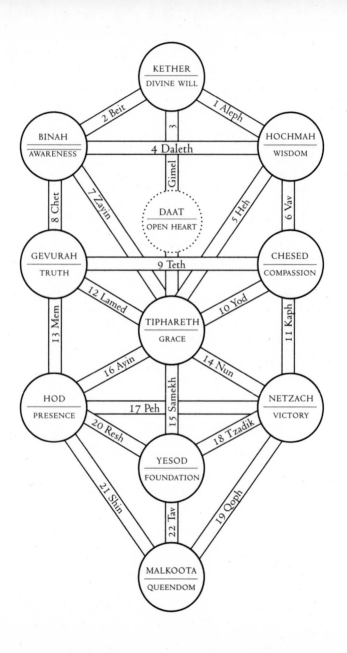

LETTER	NAME	GEMA-TRIA	LETTER	NAME	GEMA-TRIA
א	Aleph	I	**ל**	Lamed	30
ב	Beit	2	**מ**	Mem	40
ג	Gimel	3	**נ**	Nun	50
ד	Daleth	4	**ס**	Samech	60
ה	Heh	5	**ע**	Ayin	70
ו	Vav	6	**פ**	Peh	80
ז	Zayin	7	**צ**	Tzadik	90
ח	Chet	8	**ק**	Qoph	I00
ט	Teth	9	**ר**	Resh	200
י	Yod	I0	**ש**	Shin	300
כ	Kaph	20	**ת**	Tav	400

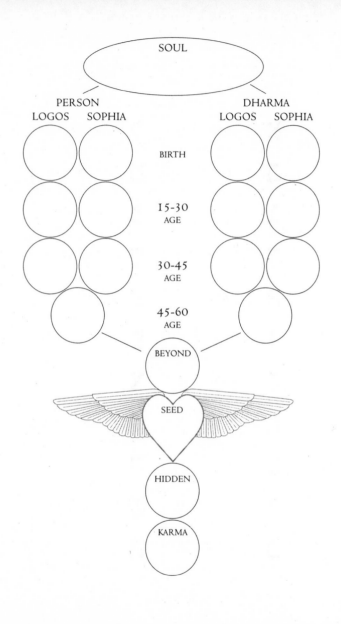

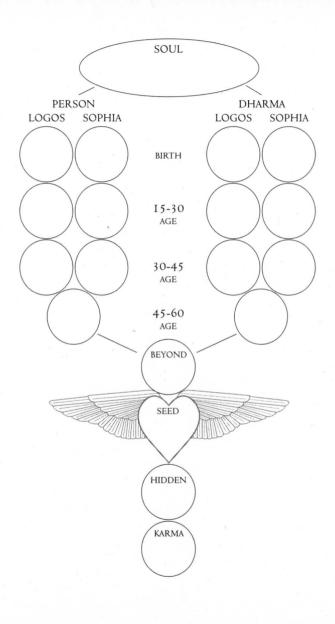

MAY THE HEAVENLY SOURCE
BLESS YOU AND KEEP YOU
MAY THE GRACIOUS SHM
SHINE AND VIBRATE THROUGH YOU
AND GIVE YOU PEACE

SHLAMA ALAKHOOM